*Guillory*

*Keep up the good work!*

# TRANSFORMING YOUR LIFE FROM GOOD TO GREAT: DAILY NUGGETS OF WISDOM

## BY WILLIE SPEARS

### EDITED BY ERIN HICKS-CHEEK

*9/14*

Copyright © 2014
Willie Spears
All rights reserved.
ISBN: 1495963152
ISBN-13: 9781495963155

I DEDICATE THIS BOOK TO THE MEN
AND WOMEN
WHO INSPIRED ME TO GROW AND HELPED ME
ALONG THE WAY.

FRONT COVER PHOTO BY VALARIE CASE
BACK COVER PHOTO BY JEAN LEE JACKSON
COVER DESIGN BY ERIN HICKS–CHEEK

# Praise for *Transforming Your Life from Good to Great Daily Nuggets of Wisdom*

"Willie Spears tells a great story and at the end you realize you have learned something valuable for your life's journey."

-Allen E. Bird, CEO, Northwestern Oklahoma State University Foundation, Alva, OK

"After reading *Transforming Your Life from Good to Great,* it is evident that everyone, on all levels, will enjoy the structure, sequence, and details that are outlined from day to day and week to week... an exceptionally realistic approach... Powerful."

-Dr. Coleta N. Thomas, Georgia educator

"Willie's book is him all the way! Challenging, inspiring, convicting, informative, applicable, funny, and a great source of encouragement! The Lord has allowed him a wide range of life experiences to bring a fresh perspective to life's journey with each day's nugget. A great read for all!"

-Dave Gittings, Campus Sports Pastor & Football Chaplian, Virginia Tech

"Willie shares some important ingredients for living your life to the fullest. He illustrates the benefits of passion, persistence, and perspiration for daily moving forward to become the best version of yourself. He emphasizes how your everyday choices, big and small, impact who you are and where you can go in this world."

-Dr. Cheryl Evans, President, Northern Oklahoma College

"I recommend this book to everyone who breathes. The title could be 'From ordinary to extraordinary.' Willie Spears has masterfully crafted a resource beneficial to everyone regardless of socioeconomic status, race, religion, gender, or position. This book is for all of us."

-Tim Albin, Offensive Coordinator, Ohio University

"I wish that my grandchildren would read this book and apply it to their lives. I love it! I want to buy at least five copies!"

-Kate Hicks, retired educator and entrepreneur, ElReno, OK

"...Anyone that reads it will take away something positive from it. It is designed in a way that it can challenge anyone, any age and from any walk of life, from child to senior, new leader to top executive. The daily nuggets are valuable tools that everyone should have in their toolbox."

-Chelsea Grande, manager of Community Development, Whitecourt, Alberta, Canada

# More Praise for *Transforming Your Life from Good to Great Daily Nuggets of Wisdom*

"I have read many books in my life, but rarely has one impacted me as much as Willie Spears' new book, *Transforming Your Life from Good to Great: Daily Nuggets of Wisdom*. I love this book because it is inspirational, practical, insightful, potent, and exciting to read! This book will change your life! However, the true greatness of this work lies behind the man who wrote it. Willie Spears practices what he preaches, he lives the life that he writes about. After reading this book, and doing what it says, I promise that your life will go from good to great!"

**Lee Jenkins, Pastor, Ministry Leader, Author, Speaker, Coach**
**Eagles Nest Church & Fellowship of Christian Athletes, Atlanta, GA**

"Willie's book *Transforming Your Life from Good to Great* is on point. It happens to be exactly what I'm trying to do. This is God speaking to me."

**-Neefy Moffet, Former Tampa Bay Buccaneer (NFL)**

"As both a parent and a teacher, I love this book. What Willie has provided parents and teachers with is a book that is relevant to children and students of all ages. This book serves as a resource for students as they begin to formulate their own life plan. If read daily, this book has the potential and the power to change a lot of lives!"

**-Jocelyn Corley, English teacher, Arkansas City, Kansas**

"After reading Willie's book, I am excited about going from good to great in my business, in my personal life, and my health. I have made some serious decisions based on the information found in this great resource. I am buying a few copies for my friends, so that they can go to the next level in their lives."

**-Ka Lai Woods, Tastefully Simple team mentor, Kansas City, MO**

"Every young person in America should have the opportunity to hear Willie Spears speak and to read his books. Truly an anointed man of God that has the unique ability to connect to young people regardless of their social, economic, and ethical background. A fired up and inspired man of God."

**-Terry Ross, bank president, Alva, OK**

"Willie Spears is a great motivator and storyteller who knows how to grab his audiences' attention. *Transforming Your Life from Good to Great* is a book that is very relevant today and for years to come. I will personally use his Nuggets of Wisdom to inspire my staff to become the best educators they can be."

**-Anthony Brock, Principal, St. Jude Educational Institute, Montgomery, AL**

# CONTENTS

# How to Use This Book

I believe this book has the potential to change your life. This is more than a book; it is a guide to a month-long journey that will enable you to transform your life from good to great. The average life span is 70 years, or in smaller increments, 25,550 days. A typical year consists of 365 days, and each month is an average of 30 days. This book is designed to be read daily through a typical work week, leaving the weekend for reflection and application. You should complete the book in less than 30 days.

The book is divided into 20 small chapters, or nuggets. I suggest you read one nugget per day, at the same time each day. This way you will have 24 hours to ponder what you've read. We usually read books with the goal of completing the book, so we read fast, often missing the author's point.

This is not a novel or a short story. This is a book that you savor. This is a crock-pot, not a microwave. A two mile run, not the hundred yard dash. Take your time and read each nugget with application in mind. Ask yourself: what does this look like? How can I apply this? Does this apply to my life?

Don't just read this book. Give it a high five, throw it down, toss it up, smile, laugh, cry. Interact with it. Highlight, underline, circle, and doodle. Put your two cents in. Add. Take away. Make it your book. Personalize it. If you look at my favorite Bible or any of my favorite books, you will see my fingerprints on them. Not my actual fingerprints, but my personal touch in the markings on the pages. A short pencil is better than a long memory. Take notes and make notes.

Each day has a goal and purpose. Some days are light; others are heavy. We start with something easy each week and end with something about sports- sometimes serious, sometimes fun. Tuesday through Thursday, the topics are heavy and thought provoking.

At the end of the week, the goal is to pick two of the five items addressed and make an effort to go from good to great in those two areas. After deciding which two areas you are going to focus on, formulate a plan of action. Then, ask yourself, "What I am going to do each day to accomplish my goal?" Be sure to chart your progress and reward yourself periodically.

The best way to chart your progress is to first define it. Secondly, keep track by marking happy faces on a calendar for good days and sad faces for days you missed the mark.

The beauty of this book is its endless opportunities. You can read it over and over again, gaining something different each time. You can use this book as an icebreaker for meetings on your job each day. After reading it once and choosing two nuggets a week to work on, re-read it, selecting two different nuggets per week. You can post the daily quotes and memorize them, or just use this resource as a challenge.

I am enjoying the good life, but I am ready to go from good to great. How about you?

# Introduction

LG Corporation is based out of South Korea. They make electronics, chemicals, and operate other companies in 80 different countries. You may have a cell phone or refrigerator manufactured by LG. Their slogan is, "Life is good."

Is your life good? I bet your life is good in at least one area. If you don't believe your life is good, I challenge you to find the good. It is all a matter of perspective. Someone has it better than you, and someone has it worse. However, we all have it good in some way.

One of my friends just returned from a trip to Africa. He spent time with a family who lived in a mud hut and ate small portions of food each day. Although they did not have a lot to eat or drink, they told him, "Life is good."

One of my football players took a recruiting trip to a Division I university, and after seeing the living quarters and the cafeteria, he said, with a heavy southern drawl, "This here good living, Coach." When I go back to my home town of Panama City, Florida, I often run into old acquaintances. When we greet each other they often ask, "What's good with ya?"

So I ask you, *what's good with you?* It is so easy to find the bad, but what about the good? When my family and I spend the night at my in-laws' house, I greet my father in law by saying, "good morning." He always responds by saying, "It is a good morning." What a great attitude.

How's your attitude? My friend Jason McLeod starred in the movie *Facing the Giants.* One of my favorite lines from that movie is *"Your attitude is the aroma of your heart."* Attitude determines altitude. In other words, the height you attain in life, business, or in general is determined by your attitude. A great attitude can lead to a great life.

In 2002, I began teaching high school sophomores in a course called Life Management Skills. I wanted to let the students know what real life would be like if they made bad decisions as adolescents. So, before handing out the syllabus and going over the classroom rules, I would write one word on the board: SUCKS. This not only got their attention, it kept them on edge the entire semester.

My first lecture began with the following:

*The decisions you make today will determine your tomorrow. Life does not just happen; you have the power to make it happen. For most people, the way their life will turn out is determined by lifestyle choices. Think about your parents, uncles, aunts, and other relatives' lifestyles. Are these examples of what you envision for your life?*

*Imagine being an adult and waking up next to someone you love but don't like. Or, wanting to wake up next to someone, yet waking up alone. Imagine getting out of a bed that you want to get rid of, in a place you don't like living, surrounded by the sound of teenagers and young children who don't listen to you, much less obey. Imagine driving to a job you hate, in a car you hate more, to work for a boss you thought hated you but promoted you, which cued your coworkers to show themselves as true haters.*

*Imagine being a smoker who wants to quit but can't; a former casual drinker who now has a problem; a good person with great intentions but because of bad decisions, can't find meaningful employment. Imagine the life you always imagined, yet you have a life nothing like you imagined. The drug dealer never wanted to be a drug dealer. The bad parent never had this in mind. The law breaker never intended to break the law. It just happened. Most of our parents didn't have a plan, their lives just happened. For many of us, our birthdays just happened. We weren't planned.*

I would then ask a young man if he would have children before he got married. In each class, almost every time, the response was, "I don't know." Therein lies the problem. The young men actually did not realize that they were in full control of whether or not they fathered a child. Most of them had never considered the notion of planning for the future. At this point I would introduce them to a popular quote from Benjamin Franklin, "If we fail to plan, then we plan to fail."

If our life is not good or great, it is usually because we didn't have a plan. We just allowed it to happen. Imagine traveling with no clue of your destination and no map, or baking a cobbler without a recipe. There has to be a plan. We are all lost without a guide. What's your plan?

As a young adult, I had so many plans about what I would do as a career. In 1996, as a high school senior, I was interviewed by the Florida-based magazine *Role Models.* They asked me what I saw myself doing as a career. I answered, *"I don't see myself doing anything for a long period of time. I like a challenge. I may coach, or be an actor, or some sort of entertainer."* As it turns out, it appears I was some sort of prophet.

The Bible says that people perish because they lack vision. My father asked me to write my goals down as it says in the book of Habakkuk, and I did. Every morning when I went to brush my teeth, I would see my goals: Professional football player, Actor, Comedian, Rapper, and Director. By the age of 26, I had received compensation or an award for all of these occupations. I was well on my way to becoming an entertainer.

I landed a job as a morning radio personality on Rochester, New York's hottest hip hop station, WDKX. As I sat in a meeting with program-director Andre Marcel (Magic Johnson's college roommate) I realized the entertainment business was not for me. It was 2002, the R&B singer Ashanti was coming to town, and he had chosen me to interview her. Interviewing celebrities was not new for me, I had interviewed Sharon Stone when I was in high school, Bow Wow a few weeks before the Ashanti assignment, and spent time on CNN with Lou Waters- one of the first to anchor on the all-news network. I thought Ashanti was one of the most beautiful women in the business at the time, and interviewing her would have really been amazing. However, I didn't get the rush I thought I would.  Instead of doing the interview, I returned to Florida for a short vacation, and never returned to Rochester. I didn't know it at the time, but I had a longing to help young people.

Six years earlier, as a recent college graduate, I had gone back home to visit my high school teachers at Rutherford, my alma mater. I walked in to the assistant principal's office as she was reading an article about the superintendent of schools.  As we sat chatting, out of nowhere, she declared that I could be superintendent of schools one day. She told me that I could teach and coach for ten years, then go into administration. After twenty years of doing those jobs, I could run for superintendent of schools. I told her that I would never teach because I didn't like teachers.

Turns out, I am not a prophet.

We bring all of our experiences to every situation. Everything we have faced and experienced influences our decision making depending on the context. We are all wired differently, but most of what we are is a product of our upbringing and surroundings.

When I was growing-up, my father was in Amway, a network marketing company designed to provide families financial freedom. Part of his training was motivational tapes and books. I would listen to Zig Ziglar, Les Brown, Rich Devos, and Jay Van Andel as they talked about achieving your dreams by reaching your goals. At the age of ten, I read the book *How to Win Friends and Influence People* by Dale Carnegie. At age 13, I read *One Minute Manager* by Kenneth Blanchard and Spencer Johnson. As a result, the art of living an optimistic life, believing and achieving, working hard, and building up others is normal for me. You could say my father brainwashed me.

These events and resources helped shape the person I am today, and these are the experiences I bring to this moment.

I often take phone calls from people I've met who are seeking advice on managing an area of their life. Sometimes they merely want a sounding board or an objective point of few. There are areas in which I am proficient, and there are areas where I am not. Sometimes all I can do for them is pray. Other times, I can share a story or provide an analogy that may help. I believe there is always a way to improve our quality of life, enabling us to transform it from good to great.

- Willie Spears

THE WILLIE SPEARS EXPERIENCE

# WEEK ONE

# MONDAY

"The man who does not read good books has no advantage over the man who can't read."

Mark Twain

## SMART PEOPLE READ

Years ago, I was blessed to speak to 3,000 students in Montgomery Alabama on the campus of Alabama State University in the famous Acadome. After my speech, I decided to change out of my sweaty shirt and head to Dexter Avenue Baptist Church. I changed into a black shirt that says "Smart People Read." This was a promotional shirt that we sold to promote the first book I wrote, *Keisha's Dilemma*. As I changed clothes, I beamed with excitement because I was going to visit the church where Dr. Martin Luther King Jr. first served as pastor.

In 1954, at the age of 25, Reverend Martin Luther King Jr. followed in the footsteps of his father and grandfather and became a pastor. His first assignment as church leader began as the Pastor of Dexter Avenue Baptist Church in Montgomery, Alabama. In the basement of the church, he helped organize the Montgomery Bus Boycott. The Boycott lasted more than a year and sparked the Civil Rights Movement. I am a history buff, especially African-American history. I was so excited about the opportunity to visit the church and sit in the actual basement where the meetings occurred that changed America. At the end of the tour, they showed us a video, and I cried like a baby as I realized the magnitude of the moment.

When I walked off the street into the basement, I noticed a mural, so I took out my phone and immediately started taking pictures. The painting was beautiful and so were the items they had for display. While I continued to capture the moment, I heard a group of people coming down to the basement from the sanctuary. It was a group of senior citizens from Atlanta walking into the church basement for a tour. I really didn't want anyone else there while I was there, and I didn't want to be bothered. I was trying to unwind and relax before I got back on the road to head home.

One lady in particular started asking me questions. She was all in my business, "I like your shirt young man."

"Thank you," I said.

"So you like to read?"

"Yes, ma'am," was my reply as I tried to walk around her and get away.

She followed me. "Your shirt says 'Smart People Read.'"

"Yes, ma'am, it does," I replied.

She kept pressing, "Are you smart?"

"Ma'am, I don't know," I sighed in frustration. "I like this shirt."

She considered this. "So can you not read, or are you not smart? Which one is it?"

"I can read, lady," I retorted in the loudest whisper I could muster.

"Well, what does that sign say?" She asked as she pointed to the sign directly above my head.

I replied with great intensity as I read, "PLEASE DO NOT TAKE PIC-TURES! There are you satisfied. I read it, I can read. It says...oh. Oh. I see your point. I shouldn't be taking pictures."

She laughed and we actually made a positive connection; however, I was a little embarrassed.

The statistics on literacy in America are also embarrassing. According to the Statistic Brain Research Institute, over 75% of prisoners are illiterate. Only a third of high school students will read a book after high school. 80% of US families will not buy a book this year. 70% of adults have not visited a bookstore in the past five years. Everywhere you look, the statistics are similar. As a nation, we don't like to read, and we should be embarrassed.

I once had to grocery shop for an event at my school. One of the ingredients on my list was the seasoning thyme. I have a master's degree in education, and I am a certified teacher. I pronounced the seasoning thigh-me. I asked the Wal-Mart associate where I could find thigh-me. She asked me to repeat the name again. I assumed she was hard of hearing or I was not enunciating well enough. I repeated it slowly and loudly and gave her a visual aide. I pointed to my thigh and then I pointed to myself by putting my index finger in the middle of my chest, "Thigh-Me, ma'am, thigh (pause) me, thigh-me." She asked if she could read my grocery list. I showed her the paper and I pointed to the word thyme. She said, "You mean thyme" (pronounced time).

"Oh, yes ma'am, thyme," I responded.

Why didn't I know the correct pronunciation of that word? Am I not smart? Do I not cook enough? Most likely, the word "thyme" was unfamiliar to me because I don't spend much "time" reading cook books. In order to gain knowledge in any area, it is essential that we read. To learn more about sports, read a sports magazine. To learn more about seasonings with funny spellings, read *Southern Living*. Whatever our area of interest, to learn more, we must read more.

When I am blessed with the opportunity to speak to young people, I always ask them how they feel about reading. But first, I ask them what they want to be when they grow up. The answers range from professional athlete, to entertainer, engineer, and video game designer. I then ask the group, "What are you reading?" Far too often the response is silence. Crickets.

"But I know you like to read," I say. "Why aren't you reading a book?"

They fire back that reading is boring. It takes too long. They'd rather be playing a sport.

After listening to their excuses I ask, "What about text messages? Do you read those? Facebook or Instagram comments?"

The response is always a resounding "yes."

"Oh, so you do like reading!"

Like these students, so many people don't think of themselves as readers, but they spend hours reading posts on Facebook or Twitter. Many people don't consider themselves readers, but they read magazines in the beauty shop or closely follow sports scores online or in the newspaper. The first step in improving our literacy is understanding that we are already readers.

The second step is understanding the importance of reading. Many people think it is possible to become a great success without becoming a person who reads. Students, especially, think that if they become a professional entertainer or athlete, they won't need to read.

"Tell me this," I challenge students, "how can you be a rapper and not read your lyrics? How can you design video games on the computer and not have a lot of reading to do? How can you be a professional athlete and trust someone else to read your contract for you?"

I tell them about contract disputes between top recording artists and their managers. In most cases, these disputes are the result of the artists' failure to carefully read the contract. The same fate often befalls famous athletes who have had contract disputes with their teams and agents. Frequently the talented individual did not read their contract. My guess is because they don't like reading.

In the early 1800's, it was illegal for slaves to learn how to read. A woman named Sophia Auld started teaching a young slave named Frederick Douglass how to read. When her husband found out, he asked her to discontinue the reading lessons. After that, Douglass began teaching himself how to read. He had such a thirst for knowledge and education that he was willing to risk his life. This thirst would eventually lead to his freedom and the freedom of others.

There is power in reading. When we read a book, we escape to another world. When we read, we bring our own interpretation to each word and each page. Reading is therapeutic. Not only is it a great way to pass the time, reading expands the mind. It is a catalyst for creativity, invention, and contemplation. In short, reading makes us think.

Have you thought about picking up a book and reading it, or ordering a book on your phone, tablet, Nook, or Kindle? Library cards are free of charge, and many libraries also lend e-books. If you already read, have you thought about reading more or expanding your interest area?

I try to read a book a month. Why? Reading is exercise for my brain. In 2009, *Time* magazine published a story about an ongoing study conducted by researchers at the University of Minnesota. They have discovered that the greater a person's language skills, the more resistant they are to brain disorders such as dementia and Alzheimer's disease later in life. By studying a group of over 600 Roman Catholic nuns, researchers have found that the women who had strong reading and speaking skills in their youth, and continued to read and occupy their minds with exercises such as crossword puzzles throughout middle and old age, were still mentally acute and productive well into their eighties, nineties and beyond! My body needs exercise to be its best, and my brain does as well. Just as taking care of our bodies when we're young can pay off for us when we are older, taking care of our brain will also pay off in the long term.

The good news is you're reading now! In my book, that makes you smart because SMART PEOPLE READ.

# TUESDAY

"The key is not to prioritize what's on your schedule, but to schedule your priorities."

Stephen R. Covey

## PRIORITIES

I publicly preach faith, family, and football as my priorities; in that order. What I have learned is that action speaks louder than words. During the fall, football takes most of my time; during the spring and summer, I am occupied with football, writing, and speaking. In order to keep my priorities in order, I had to plan time for my faith and my family.

I made a personal vow to be in church every Sunday and to read my Bible every day. Although I am currently struggling with my prayer life, there was a time when praying was a scheduled priority. I would wake up an hour early to pray for thirty minutes and read for thirty minutes.

I schedule time for my family as well. My wife and I go on scheduled vacations twice a year. Sometimes the trip is a work vacation. Last year, we went to Hawaii to speak at a youth camp and to enjoy one another's company on the island. We also schedule time for the family. At least twice a week, we eat together as a family. We attend church together as a family weekly, and we take at least one family vacation each year.

The schedule helps me keep my priorities in line. I believe priorities are the recipes for the ingredients of our lives. If we put what we actually do in a bowl and just mix it up, we may not enjoy the result. However, our end product is much better if we prioritize and put our ingredients in the bowl in the right order. In life, as in cooking, we get out what we put in.

Just as it is important to add our ingredients in the correct order, it is also important to choose the right ingredients. Truthfully, I don't always want to go on vacation, or go to church, or read the Bible, or get home to eat with the family; however, I try to think of the end result. What would happen if I neglected these priorities? Ingredients are important. If I smoke, I may get lung cancer; but if I exercise, I may enjoy good health. If I put my faith and my family first, I will enjoy life more. The correct ingredients can produce a delicious cake; the incorrect ingredients make a product that leaves a bad taste in your mouth.

My wife makes a tremendous pound cake. Once, we had a huge argument about something important. I was so upset that I decided to go stay with a friend for a while and packed my belongings in my truck. I continued to give her an earful as I walked down the stairs with my bulky television with the tube in the back. As I hefted the T.V., grunting between rants because it was heavy, my wife came up behind me and put a piece of her famous pound cake in my mouth.

The moist cake muffled my volume, making my next point literally mute. As the block of sweetness melted in my sassy mouth, I somehow decided to return my television to the den. Subsequently, I moved all my belongings back in the house.

Just kidding, that didn't really happen. However my wife does make an amazing pound cake. The ingredients are as follows:

1 ½ cups (3 sticks) butter, softened

One 8-ounce package cream cheese, softened

3 cups sugar

6 large eggs

3 cups of cake flour, sifted twice

Pinch of salt

1 teaspoon vanilla extract

1 teaspoon almond extract

If you put these items in a bowl and mix them together they will become one. If you then apply heat, they will rise and become something totally different.

The same is true with the ingredients of our life. We are the product of all our priorities. When a person's priorities are combined, the resulting batter is a person. When heat is applied in the form of adversity, the real person rises up.

If I asked you what the ingredients of your life were you would probably say: family, faith, friends, country, or something along those lines. Ingredients are active agents. What do you actually do? What are your disciplines? What is your behavior? What verbs summarize your life? If someone were to secretly follow you for one week each month, for four months, what would they discover about you?

At the age of 15, a young man I know was smoking weed, skipping school, and carrying a gun. I told him that those ingredients would add up to jail. Sadly, I was right. He is currently 25 years old and serving a life sentence.

If you don't exercise, and you don't eat healthy foods, you will gain unhealthy weight. If you drink too much alcohol, you risk making poor decisions and eventual organ damage. If you lie, the truth will catch up with you. If you don't get proper rest, fatigue will have a negative effect on your health. If you hang out with people who break the law, you may get in trouble. The correlation between these actions and results seems like common sense.

I am often visited by former students who are pregnant and in disbelief about their situation. I ask, "Um, did you have unprotected sex?"

They respond, "Yeah, but..."

"But what? If you have unprotected sex there is a chance you can get pregnant."

People in general, young people especially, tend to think that they can always buck the odds. They just know that they will be the exception to the rule. However, it is short-sighted for us to think that we will be the one person for whom 4 + 4 equals 5. Our ingredients add up to our product. We must choose the ingredients that will ensure the future that we want to create.

We have car insurance in case we are in an accident. We wear our seatbelts in case we are in an accident. Why are we more careful with our cars, than with the direction of our lives? Smart people think about the future. Foolish people make decisions in the moment, based on their current situation. Smart people plan their futures and act on the plans. Foolish people don't plan and can only react to events as they happen.

What are your priorities? How do they line up with your beliefs? Are the activities you are involved in everyday leading somewhere, or are you just surviving? Remember, if we fail to plan, we plan to fail. People who don't have a plan find themselves saying: how did I get here?

Let's take Pat. Pat is twenty-four years old, has two girlfriends, one daughter, and lives at home with his mother. According to society's standards, he is a good person. He goes to church, he loves his mother, and he is not angry, rude, or disrespectful.

Pat doesn't think people should judge him based on his appearance. He believes his tattoos, hair, clothing, and piercings are just the cover, not the whole book. Pat uses drugs on a weekly basis; he does not have a job but has a car and a few pairs of new shoes. During the week, he likes to play video games and watch music videos. Pat is an avid sports fan and roots for his hometown team. He eats fast food and snacks all day. Although his friends sell drugs and carry guns, he does not. Pat dropped out of high school because he was too old to play basketball his senior year, and he felt everyone gave up on him.

When we evaluate the ingredients of his life where do we see Pat in the next 10 years?

Now let's look at Doug, or Douglas, as he introduces himself in some circles. Douglas is also twenty-four years old, has two girlfriends, one daughter, and lives at home with his mother. He has a plan to break up with one of the girls and get his own place. According to society's standards, he is a good person. He goes to church, he loves his mother, and he is not angry, rude, or disrespectful. He feels like he needs to make some changes in his life, so he has started spending time with one of the men in the church who is mentoring him.

Doug doesn't think people should judge him on his appearance. He believes his tattoos, hair, clothing, and piercings are just the cover, not the whole book. Doug does not sell drugs, but he uses them on a weekly basis. He does not have a job but has a car and a few pairs of new shoes. Deep down, he feels bad for using one of his girlfriends to buy him things, so he has made a promise to himself to apply for a job every day until he gets one.

During the week, he likes to play video games and watch music videos. Doug is an avid sports fan and roots for his hometown team. He eats fast food and snacks all day, and although his friends sell drugs and carry guns, he does not.

Doug knows that his lifestyle is going to get him in trouble one day, so he is trying to distance himself from people who make bad choices. Doug dropped out of high school because he was too old to play baseball his senior year of high school, and he felt that everyone gave up on him. He volunteers with the little league park down the street from his house in an effort to not give up on kids in the neighborhood.

When we evaluate the ingredients of his life, where do we see Doug in the next 10 years?

Both of these young men are missing a recipe for the ingredients of their lives. They haven't considered what is important to them. They don't know what their priorities are. Pat does not have a plan at all; he is just living day to day. Doug is trying to formulate a plan, but without defined priorities, it is difficult to make a plan for living. It is hard to follow a recipe, without a list of ingredients.

Knowing what your priorities are will shape your life. It will help you make tough decisions with your family, with your business, and in society. When we do not have defined priorities we tend to use emotions or the way we feel to make decisions. This is dangerous.

What is more dangerous is not knowing what your priorities are. If you want to know your priorities, take notes on where you spend your time and money. This will reveal what is important to you. Time is our most valuable asset. What are you doing with your time? There are twenty-four hours in a day, and fourteen hundred, forty minutes in a day. What are you doing with all that time? This will tell you what your priorities are.

Once you define what is important to you, you can then begin to prioritize. Soon, you will have a recipe for the future you are longing for, and it will be time to start baking.

# Wednesday

"You never really learn much from hearing yourself speak."

George Clooney

## Two Ears One Mouth

I have never met a person with two mouths and one ear. Every person I have ever met has two ears and one mouth. I have never met Evander Holyfield, but I hear (pun intended) he is missing part of his ear.

Why did God create us with one mouth and two ears? The obvious answer is so that we can listen twice as much as we speak, but it is deeper than that. I believe another reason we have two ears and one mouth is because we should listen before we speak. As a leader, it is especially important to listen before you speak, to hear what everyone has to say before you open your mouth. This does not mean you will change your mind or that their opinion will alter your decision, but no one wants to follow a leader who does not have time to listen to others.

When I was growing up, my father would ask me if I wanted to wash the dishes or mow the grass. Like most young people, I chose the path of least resistance, or the easier of the two. I said, "Dad I'll wash the dishes."

"Good," he would respond, "when you finish with the dishes get out there and mow that grass." He made me feel like I was part of the decision making process.

As a leader, the words that come out of your mouth are significant. Words have gotten leaders fired, and have caused leaders to lose support and funding. The Bible says that life and death are in the power of the tongue. Biologically the tongue is the strongest muscle in the body. As a child, I remember hearing, "Sticks and stones may break my bones, but words will never hurt me." This is a cute little saying, but it is false.

Words build up, tear down, inspire, demoralize, and move us in one direction or another, and words mean so much more coming from a leader. The father, mother, owner, president, boss, manager, principal, coach, supervisor and pastor have to really think before speaking. Our words can scar a person for life.

As parents, we must be very careful with what we say around our children. They are recording devices. They will say what you say. One of my friends is a Division I football coach in the Big 12 conference. He talked to me one day about the language he uses as a coach. He explained that he used to talk one way as a coach and another way at home. Then, one day it all changed.

He and his wife had their first child, a beautiful girl. When his daughter began to speak, her first word was not mommy. Her first word wasn't daddy. Her first word was the "F-word." He said that she said it loud and clear. He realized that his wife had brought her to practice several times, and that she had probably heard him say *that* word several times. He decided to monitor his language.

What usually comes out of our mouth is what we have built up inside of us. Therefore, we must be careful what we allow to come in to our minds. There is an old Children's Bible song titled "Be Careful, Little Eyes." It says:

> *O be careful little eyes what you see.*
> *O be careful little ears what you hear.*
> *O be careful little hands what you do.*
> *O be careful little feet where you go.*

This is great advice. It is hard to repeat something you've never heard or seen. When we hear and see things over and over it becomes normal. Remember when you would hear a four letter word and your ears would perk up? Remember when you would hear the "N-word" and your ears would perk up? There was a time when seeing two women kiss was abnormal. What has happened is that we have been inundated with immoral behavior. This behavior has forced itself on us, and has become the norm.

I have lived in many different parts of the country, and I have noticed differences in tolerance depending on the culture of the area.  I've lived in a city where it is customary for a women to have on a bikini top in a local store. In two cities, I saw zero biracial children and no interracial couples. In other cities, half the population seems to be in a relationship with someone of a difference race. In one place we lived, half the boys carried pocket knives. In another place, one of my players was expelled from school for carrying a pocket knife. At one school, the students would leave in the middle of the day to go to a rap concert, and no one in authority had a problem with it. In another city, students did not come to school on the first day of hunting season, and no one in authority had a problem with it.

These examples are not necessarily right or wrong, but they do illustrate the differences that exist from one community to another. I mention them to remind us that our norms are based on...our norms. Where I live, there seem to be a lot of Dollar General stores popping up. There also seem to be a lot of Hooters restaurants closing. Through research, I found that Hooters annual sales have not risen in six years.

In 1983, when Robert Brooks and Ed Droste founded Hooters, there was no World Series of Poker on ESPN. Gambling was considered a taboo addiction suited only for the low-life. In 1983, pornography was not readily available or accessible through smart phones. There was a fine line between "good" girls and "naughty" girls. In 2013, that line is not blurred; it's gone. The gimmick that made Hooters a hit with so many male sports fans is the fact that they could look at a woman's bosom without offending her.

Think about it; beer, sports, and women in tight shirts. In 1983, television shows like *Dallas, Dynasty*, and the *Love Boat* were the closest things you could get without being considered a pervert. Now we have women playing football in their underwear and half-naked women advertising food and cell phones. We have been desensitized. Hooters is almost G-rated these days. A male sports fan can go to any sports bar and see girls in tight shirts serving beer. Times have changed, but even though we have two eyes, we must be careful what we allow them to see.

Our behavior has adjusted to society's norms. This is especially prevalent in our choice of music. Music is the most powerful art form known to man. One artist said "Music make you lose control." I have found this statement to have great truth. The song "I'll Fly Away" brings tears to many eyes because it is sung at funerals. Some people hear that song and instantly water begins to pour from their eyes.

Since the passing of both of my grandparents, some of the songs from their funerals cause me to well up. Eartha Mae Thomas, the younger of the two, died at the age of 76. My cousin Ricardo sang the song "I'd Rather Have Jesus than Silver and Gold" by Kirk Franklin's choir at the funeral. My goodness, you talk about emotional.

For two years, I did an independent study of music, and my findings told an amazing story. Have you noticed that you know songs that you don't like? You may find yourself singing or humming tunes that are far from your favorite. My daughter knew her alphabet at the age of sixteen months, not because she was smart or gifted, but because it was set to music.

Music is the only medium that crosses both hemispheres of the brain. Your brain records information without your permission. The largest part of the brain is the cerebral cortex, which is divided into the left and right hemispheres. The left side of your brain deals with details or analytic thinking, such as verbal or mathematical problems. The right brain processes information in an instinctive, direct, and creative manner.

Music has the potential to change a person's state of consciousness. When using music therapy, it is possible to shift a person's perception of time and reality. Music has been called the universal language. There are songs in all genres that are positive and uplifting or just good and enjoyable. Some say that music reflects society, and that may be true. But, instead of glorifying the negative things in society, why not glorify the positive? The reason is because negative, evil, bad topics sell. No one wants to hear a song about a man taking care of his family and contributing to society by mentoring or volunteering. We would rather hear a song about someone having relationship problems, or hurting someone, or breaking the law. If we look at different genres, it is easy to see the negative messages promoted in music.

Country music glorifies the use and abuse of alcohol from Hank Williams's 1950 song "There's a Tear in My Beer" to the 2013 song "It Ain't the Whiskey" by Gary Allan. Hip Hop music promotes drug use, violence, and boldly disrespects women. A chart topping song in 2014 is "Gunplay" by Lil Wayne and Rick Ross. Its content resembles a hip hop classic from twenty years ago produced by Dr. Dre. In 1994, Snoop Doggy Dogg released the song "Gin and Juice" with the Parental Advisory Explicit Content label affixed to the case. This label was introduced the year before as the result of pressure from the Parents Music Resource Center (PMRC). The PMRC was formed in 1985 and had success in Washington due to the influence of the members.

This group targeted all artists from Prince to Cindy Lauper. However, it became easy for them to target rap and rock groups because of their controversial content. Rock music is not as popular as it once was, but if you search the internet for the top songs of yesterday and today you can see how the music affects culture. Pop music promotes vanity and greed, which leads to low self-esteem and crime. R&B music promotes all sorts of sexual behavior, never addressing the risks that come with this behavior.

Music has the potential to create a culture. When my children were small, we didn't put them to sleep with loud music like "Welcome to the Jungle" by Guns and Roses or "Are you Ready for Some Football" by Hank Williams, Jr. However, those are great songs to play in a high school stadium on Friday night before a football game. The lullabies we played for Tayelor and Kenneth would not get our team pumped for the game.

Two ears one mouth. Be careful what goes in, and monitor what comes out. The company we keep, the music we listen to, and the resources we digest are the ingredients that make up who we are. As a leader, you are responsible for your followers. You can only regurgitate what you have inside. As adults, we have the ability to censor and separate good and bad information. Some bad information can prove useful as a cautionary teaching tool when trying to reach a particular audience.

The danger is when negative resources are digested by young people who can't tell the difference between reality and ridiculous. Music is not real. Movies are not real. When I was five years old, I believed in Santa Claus. I was articulate enough to prove to you that Santa was real. I had the proof of presents under the Christmas tree and a picture I had taken with him at the mall. However, ten years later, at the age of fifteen, I felt foolish believing in Santa Claus. How in the world can a man fly all around the word on a sleigh drawn by reindeer? At the age of fifteen, I thought I knew everything about life and what it takes to be a man. Ten years later, at the age of twenty-five, I realized I was 100% wrong. At twenty-five I got married, and I was sure I knew what it would take to have a successful marriage, but ten years later, at the age of thirty-five, I realize I had no clue.

My point is this: we live, and learn, and hopefully mature with age. Young people have trouble deciphering between fantasy and reality, and so do many adults. As a leader you have the responsibility of leading in thought, word, and deed. Remember, you get out what you put in.

# THURSDAY

"Learn how to separate the majors and the minors."

Jim Rohn

## DON'T MAJOR IN MINORS

There are issues we must deal with in every area of life. There are issues in marriage, business, family, religion, and society. However, not all issues are major. If every issue becomes major, nothing will be accomplished. How will you know which issue to address first. When will the issues cease to exist? If you are always complaining about an issue, who will want to talk to you or work with you? In marriage, is not putting the cap on the toothpaste a major issue? What about the toilet seat? How do you deal with your spouse never taking the trash out?

When looking for a wife, I had about three major criteria. I wanted a Christian woman with a college degree, who had no addictions, and came from a good family. With that being said, I had to do some investigating to figure out if my future bride met these standards. Almost everyone is a Christian, and most believe they come from a good family. Those were the issues that were important to me, but everyone is different. I believe you have to do what works for you. What is a major issue for you?

Notice this: raising children, finances, physical appearance, or past experiences were not major issues for me. I believe the way we find our spouse in America is flawed. We date, and date, and date trying to figure out what we want in our future spouse. I believe we know at the age of thirteen what we want in a husband or wife. We want someone to love and respect us. Someone we are attracted to that will support us as we support them. Almost half of the marriages in our society end in divorce, and the statistics are worse when it comes to long-term non-legally-binding relationships.

There are many variables in creating healthy relationships in every area of life. The most important variable is self-love. If you love yourself and know who you are it will guide your decision making. As we focus on not majoring in minors, we have to take each aspect of our life and figure out what are the major points of interest and what is not so major. From home, to school, to work, to church we have to ask those questions. Many people leave their home, or school, or job, or church because of minor issues. No relationship, occupation, or church is perfect because humans are involved.

I have attended many different churches, and I have taken several religion courses. My university didn't offer theology as a minor, but I took every course available. Some of my friends are really loyal to their denomination or church type. When it comes to church, I have three major issues, and the rest are not very important to me. I believe that Jesus was born of a virgin. I believe Jesus died on the cross and rose from the dead, and I believe he is part of the trinity. The rest are minor issues for me. The order of service, the distribution of funds, the music, the time and day of service, the different auxiliaries or ministries, titles, and church mission are all minor details.

Majoring in these minor details is counterproductive. Often, we focus on minor issues that involve human flaws. For example, my cousin is a liar. From my dealings with him, I don't think he can help it. If he has on a red shirt, and you ask him what color it is, he will say it is blue. He will try to say red, but the word red won't come out of his mouth.

My mother called me once, and from the time I said hello, I could tell that she was upset. She said, "He lied to me; I can't believe he just lied to my face. How could he?"

"Who, Mamma?" I asked.

She told me his name (I can't use his name. If I did, he would just lie and say the story is not true), and I said, "Come on, Mamma, that's what he does. He lies. Liars lie. Tiger Woods hits golf balls, Oprah talks, Lebron slam dunks, and Cousin 'Joe,' lies." I told my mother that it was her fault for expecting something different. She was majoring in minors.

You can't get upset with an Owl for saying *Whooo*. That's what he *do*! When my wife and I were dating, I came by her house to pick her up for a formal event. I was about 45 minutes early, and the event was fifteen minutes away. I knocked on the door expecting her to answer and get in the car. Instead, her mother answered and invited me in. Her parents gave me a glass of juice, and I sat on the couch and talked with them for about twenty minutes as we watched television. I then got up, thanked them for the juice, and went to sit in the car. Ten minutes later, her dad opened the door and said, "You think sitting in that car is going to make her move faster? You might as well come back in the house."

I learned early on that my wife doesn't have a sense of urgency when it comes to being on time. If she were writing a book, she could probably write two hundred pages on how I can't shut up and leave an event. She could use actual examples of her waiting and waiting and waiting for me to be quiet and get in the car. We are both flawed in different ways because we are human. However, these are not major issues.

It would be foolish of my wife to be upset with me for talking too much. That's what I do. That's who I am. As my wife and I start our second decade of marriage, we are both learning to compromise. Over Thanksgiving 2013, we went to see the movie *The Best Man Holiday*; it turned out to be an excellent movie. I usually don't go to the movies, and if I do, it is with my wife and kids to see a children's show. In the film, Harold Perrineau plays a private school head master named Julian Murch who is married to a former stripper, who is now his assistant at the school. In the film, her character is questioned when a video surfaces from her past. His friends start to tease him about her former life, and every time he tried to correct them or stop them they would say: *Well, you did marry a stripper.*

It is what it is. Have you heard that? We are who we are. Why argue with your husband for drinking too much if he drank too much when you all were dating? Why argue with your wife for being lazy if she's always been lazy? People only change if and when they want to change. If the issue is major, then approach it. If it is minor, let it go.

When dealing with conflict, make sure you are not passive or aggressive. Sometimes we can be over-the-top in our approach. We allow our emotions to get the best of us, and this is usually the worst approach. On the other hand, we don't want to be passive or a door mat. When we allow people to run us over, nothing gets accomplished.

The best way to handle conflict is to be assertive. We need to be direct and to the point, confident in our behavior, assertive. When we tackle only major issues, people listen. When we tackle every minor issue, they start to tune us out.

Don't major in minors. Let it go.

# FRIDAY

"An early-morning walk is a blessing for the whole day."

Henry David Thoreau

## EXERCISE

One of the best ways to transform your life from good to great is to improve your health. You can do this by eating right and exercising. The first step is to set realistic goals and decide your purpose for exercising. Some exercise to lose weight, others to gain muscle. Others may exercise to improve the condition of their heart and to prevent cardiovascular problems. Believe it or not, some people exercise because they enjoy it.

After defining a purpose for physical activity, you must follow healthy eating habits to ensure results. The goal is to have a lifestyle change. I could give you a diet to follow and have you count your calories, but these methods are not practical. We often look at people who have lost a lot of weight in a short period of time and are amazed with their before and after pictures. However, when they return to their normal eating habits and lifestyle, they also return to their normal size.

Exercise alone is not enough to improve your health. Here is a practical nutrition guide:

1. Choose one unhealthy beverage you will almost never consume: alcohol, coffee, soda, or tea.

2. Match your water intake with whatever beverage you drink.

3. Match your bad snacks with fruit.

4. Eat three meals a day

5. Eat vegetables everyday

6. Exercise 5 days a week

You don't have to drink anything nasty or prepare certain meals. Just follow the above list and you will live a healthier life. Lazy or unhealthy people cost the nation over 150 billion dollars a year according to most publications. Unhealthy people are not as happy; they can't work as hard and/or as long. Unhealthy people can't stand for long periods of time, have to take more breaks from activity, usually have lower self-esteem, and contribute less to society.

Although there is nothing wrong with joining a gym, buying new shoes, or hiring a trainer, these changes are not necessary to improve your health. It is easy to exercise. The hard part is how, when, and where. How do you know what type of exercises to do? When is the best time to exercise? Where will you exercise?

For starters you should always have a pair of athletic shoes in your automobile. You must define exercise by doing anything active where your heart rate goes up. A sedentary lifestyle means you aren't moving. An active lifestyle means you are moving. We just want to move. Some days I work out for two hours, and some days I work out for less than 10 minutes. The idea is to do something active. Having a pair of shoes in your car will help. Go for a walk at a good pace if the opportunity presents itself.

You could walk around the mall, walk while your kids are at little league practice, walk during your lunch break, or go for a walk when you get off work or out of church. Exercising does not have to be an event.

Thoreau suggests walking first thing in the morning. Great suggestion. This way you get it out of the way. Wake up thirty minutes earlier, have your clothes and shoes at the foot of the bed along with your headphones and get to walking. Come home, shower, and start your day.

Don't overdo it, don't under do it, be like Nike and Just Do It.

If you want to look better: Exercise.

If you want to feel better: Exercise.

If you want live better: Exercise.

If you want to last longer: Exercise.

If you want to live longer: Exercise.

If you want more sleep: Exercise.

If you want less stress: Exercise.

If you want to be your best: Exercise.

# WEEKEND APPLICATION

The goal is to pick two of the five items we discussed this week and make an effort to go from good to great in that area. After deciding the two on which you wish to focus, formulate a plan of action. Then ask yourself, *What am I going to do each day to accomplish my goal?* Be sure to chart your progress and reward yourself periodically.

## Monday- Smart People Read

We talked about the importance of reading. Go ahead and choose a book to read when you finish this one. Maybe you are a person of faith and want to read the Bible more. Reading is an excellent way to take your life from good to great.

## Tuesday- Priorities

Most of us say our priorities are one thing, but our actions speak louder than those words. Can you improve your priorities? What are you spending your money on? Where are you spending your time? What is number one in your life? What is most important?

## Wednesday- Two Ears One Mouth

How can you listen more? How can you talk less? Do you need to do a better job monitoring what comes out of your mouth? One way to do this is by monitoring what goes in.  If you allow garbage in, you will experience garbage coming out.

## Thursday- Don't Major in Minors

Is it that big a deal? Is it a major issue? If it is not, let it go. It is not worth the stress and the drama that come with worrying. Stand firm on major issues, don't sweat the rest. Choose your battles. You can't fight them all.

## Friday-Exercise

Do you love your family? If you do, do what it takes to live longer. Exercise. If your goal is to take part in a physical activity five times a week, you will definitely make three. Getting your heart rate up will increase your quality of life.

# Transforming Your Life from Good to Great

# Daily Nuggets of Wisdom

# WEEK TWO

# MONDAY

"One body many members"

1 Corinthians 12:12

## KNOW YOUR ROLE

As a young boy, I spent time acting in church and school plays. Acting came naturally to me, and I enjoyed it. In college, I took acting classes and actually won the People's Choice Award a couple of times for my roles in two different productions. At one point, I actually considered acting as a profession.

I was playing Arena Football for the Columbus War Dogs in Columbus, Georgia, about an hour and forty-five minute drive from Atlanta. I set up a meeting with acting coach Nicole Rubenstein on one of our days off from football practice. I had no idea what to expect, and I was a little nervous. Nicole asked me to read over lines for a commercial and perform a monologue. When I finished, she gave me a big smile. I reciprocated the gesture as she motioned for me to take a seat.

She asked me how badly I wanted to become an actor. Honestly, I had not thought about it. At the time, all I wanted to do was play football, I was just trying this acting thing out. She then described the life of a full time actor. She told me the story of David Schwimmer. His family moved from New York to Los Angeles when he was very young so that he could become an actor. He graduated from a prestigious university as one of the top actors, and did everything he could to land a role in a hit movie or television show. Nothing seemed to work. He spent almost a decade as an unemployed, struggling actor. After years of small roles, he was cast as Ross Geller on NBC's sit-com *Friends*. He started acting in the early eighties and landed the role on *Friends* in 1994.

Nicole wanted to know if I was willing to be homeless, broke, rejected, and ridiculed. I told her I had to think about it. However, I already knew the answer. HECK NO. David Schwimmer obviously loved acting and was in it for the love, not the money or the fame. I loved football, not acting. From that moment on, I started asking myself two questions when it came to career choices. If they never pay you, will you do it? If you won the lottery, would you quit or continue? For me, a job was something you did to make money, a career is something you love. If

I could find a way to make money doing what I loved, I would never work a day in my life.

David Schwimmer found this- as did five other young actors; six different actors playing six different roles. On the show *Friends,* David's character Ross didn't act like a clueless, struggling actor, who loved food. That was not his role. That role belonged to Matt LeBlanc, who played Joey. Jennifer Aniston, Courtney Cox, Lisa Kudrow, Matthew Perry, David, and Matt all had different roles.

To paraphrase my favorite book, there are many parts, yet one body. So the eye cannot say to the hand, "I don't need you!" The head can't say to the feet, "I don't need you!" The body is put together in such a way to give honor to every member, big and small. That way there is no division in the body, and the members would have the same concern for each other. So, if one member suffers, all the members suffer with it; if one member is honored, all the members rejoice with it.

The hit show *Friends* changed the lives of all these young actors, not just one, but all. When we all work together and master our role, the possibility of success is endless. When we learn to stay in our lane, we can exceed all expectations and reach the same destination.

I have coached many sports at the high school level, and some on the youth and college level. I enjoy the training, the structure, and the discipline required to compete at a high level. One thing coaching has taught me is how to perfect my position, in other words, stay in my lane.

Currently, I am the head football coach at Escambia High School. Escambia is the alma mater of Emmitt Smith and Trent Richardson, two of the greatest high school running backs in the history of the game. Emmitt is the National Football League's all-time leading rusher, and Trent won two National Championships at Alabama and finished third in the Heisman Trophy race. These two celebrities visit often, and people ask me to get them an autograph. I tell them that I would love to, but that's not my lane. That's not my role.

My role is to be part of the welcoming committee when they arrive, not to be a fan. It is my job to make sure they want to come back again, and that they don't feel hounded when they visit their old high school. They should be able to relax and let their hair down. I truly feel honored when they come into my office and just hang out, no expectations, no stress; just old stories and laughs. I know my role.

As the head football coach, my role changes depending on our team needs. I am ultimately responsible for everything that happens in our program. We are a 6A school, housing over 1800 students. Our team has over 150 players competing on three different teams. John F. Kennedy quoted the Bible saying, "To whom much is given, much is expected." This job is a great responsibility, and the only way to do it well is to hire good people and let them do their job.

There are fifteen coaches on our staff: running back coach, two offensive line coaches, wide receiver coach, defensive coordinator, line-backer coach, defensive back coach, defensive line coach, and special teams coach. Those are only the varsity coaching positions. We also have a junior varsity and freshmen team. Someone has to drive the buses, wash the clothes, run the equipment room, do our team devotions, supervise study hall, raise money, run the weight room, take on the conditioning duties, paint the field, mow the grass, announce the games, take care of injuries, take care of public relations, booster club, parent liaison, etc.

I could write a book on what it takes to run a football program, but I am going to wait until we win a state championship to do that. My point is there are so many things to do. I honestly believe I would do a great job announcing the games on the Public Address System or on our television network (Escambia Gator Football Network.) I could also do a good job as team chaplain or strength and conditioning coach. However, these are not my duties. I have a job. I need to do my job, stay in my lane, and do what I am supposed to do. I purposely hire people of purpose who know more than I know- people who don't punch a clock and who enjoy adding value to the lives of others. I want to work with competent people of character as a coach and speaker, teacher and writer.

Imagine going through your day and having encounters with people who have a passion for their job. You wake up in the morning and your spouse enjoys their role, they don't try to be the man and the woman. They stay in their lane. You go into the bathroom, and sure enough, the sink, shower, and toilet know their roles. They are not confused and don't try to outshine one another by pulling double duty.

Picture yourself walking out of your bedroom, and you have two teenage children that are enjoying their teenage years. They don't think they are adults; they are comfortable in their roles as teenagers. In the perfect world, your teen would still sporadically act like a human, and even show occasional spurts of responsibility. But, they aren't rushing the maturation to adulthood. The adolescent years are full of challenges, but your teenagers are happy in their roles.

Your dog comes up to you and has that look of: I am your dog; I am not your child. I am fine with going outside and eating animal food. You do not have to rub me and pamper me all the time, for I am an animal. I know my role.

Then, you go to a fast food restaurant and the cashier is so happy to have a job and so happy to serve you. She is pleasant and so are the others around you. Imagine a harmonious world full of people who love themselves and know their roles.

I once had a job where it seemed my coworkers did not love themselves, and it caused problems. Unfortunately, we had several people who brought their problems to work. It seemed to me like many of them didn't want to be there. If they'd had their choice, they would have worked somewhere else, and it showed. There is nothing worse than dealing with a person who is unhappy with their situation.

A friend and I joked about how we wish we could do something to bring a smile to the faces of our colleagues. He mentioned getting a disc jockey and having a party. I gave him a play list: "Boot Scootin' Boogie," "Electric Slide," some Bee Gees, and Michael Jackson. I also jokingly told him that for the right price my cousin Leroy would show all the single ladies a good time, and they would come to work with a smile. My off-the-cuff joke didn't register on his moral compass. I thought it was funny. He didn't.

I would hate to be the jack-of-all-trades and master of none. Legendary Football Coach Paul Bear Bryant said we'd be amazed with how much would get done if no one cared who got the credit. Perfecting our position becomes a problem when we feel that we deserve more credit for what we do, and we believe we can do another person's job better than they can. Your time to lead will come. In the meantime, think about what kind of followers, workers, or assistants you want once you become the leader and become that.

Bloom where you're planted. Make the job you have your dream job. Be the change you wish to see in the world. Don't hate. Congratulate.

# TUESDAY

"It's takes a village to raise a child."

Hillary Clinton

## POSITIVE SUPPORT SYSTEM

In 2009, I was named Coach of the Year by three different organizations. In 2011, I was fired for not winning enough games. The support and phone calls I received after being let go shocked me. My colleagues reached out to show their support for me as a person and as a professional. Coaches from all over the south called me to check on me and show their support. When adversity hits, you find out who your friends are and who your associates are. For personal growth to occur and depression to remain dormant, we must have a positive support system.

A positive support system is made up of individuals who give you support in a positive productive way. There are different components to this system; you may find these components or characteristics in one or more people. For most of us, we will depend on a group to make up our support system. There are four major roles of a positive support system:

A Cheerleader: Someone who is in your corner and tells you that you can do it. They give you a high five. A text message of encouragement. A thumbs up, or an *'atta boy*. The cheerleader is the one that tells you that you did a great job on *American Idol* even though the entire country disagrees.

TLC: Not Tender Loving Care, but a Tough Love Coach. This component is the person who doesn't tell you what you want to hear, but tells you what you need to hear. They are the ones that tell you that you don't sing well. They encourage you to get singing lessons and work on what you believe is your gift of singing. The Tough Love Coach pairs a criticism with an appreciation in an effort to give you the information that you need.

 A Motivator: The motivator is a walking pep talk. The one that says *you can do it*! This person is a mixture of the Cheerleader and the Tough Love Coach. They say things like: if it were easy everyone would do it. They challenge you, and they push you to a place you never thought you could go. When they call you on the phone their first question is about your goal: Have you started on that book? How much money have you saved? When is the last time you used profanity? When was your last drink? You smoke today? How much do you weigh? Have you applied to any schools lately? Have you signed up for the test? Are you still dating two people? Then, before you answer, they say: *Hey! Let's get it together!*

<u>ESPN:</u> Not the sports network, but an Ear, Shoulder, Pat, and Napkin. We all need that person that will listen to us, give us a pat on the back, a shoulder to cry on, and a napkin to wipe our tears. This person does not give us advice or even try to sympathize with us. They are available for us to vent and let it all out. They allow us the freedom of vulnerability. We can tell this person anything, and they won't repeat it. They are there when we need them.

These four components, like tires on a car, give us the proper balance and help us enjoy a smooth ride. Every smooth ride has a flat at some point. When that happens, you have to trust your support system. Your support system is made up of the tools you need to get rolling again. Tools like your spare tire, your jack, and your tire iron. If they're close by, you have a chance to get back on the road faster. Your support system needs to be accessible.

Have you ever played that trust game where you fall back and the person catches you? That is a support system. I have friends and relatives who are addicted to drugs. One friend and one cousin in particular are former addicts who are currently beacons in their community. These two women were lost causes. They made decisions based on their needs, and nothing would stand in the way of them getting their next fix. However, they both changed. My children are eight and nine years old and only know them as productive citizens, as great contributors to society. How did this happen? How did these two women change from draining society of its resources to adding value to the lives of others? They both had positive support systems and firm foundations to support change.

When studying metamorphosis, I discovered that there has to be some sort of foundation, or support, in order for change to take place. When most of us think of metamorphosis we think of a caterpillar turning into a butterfly. There are various forms of this biological process. Video games and science fiction writers have shortened the term to "morph," which means *to change*. Metamorphosis is usually accompanied by a change of habitat or behavior. How does this happen? In our lives, there must be a positive support system for change to occur.

In Disney/Pixar's *A Bugs Life,* Heimlich is an obese caterpillar with tiny wings. How did this happen? Someone interrupted the caterpillar in the cocoon, administering the wrong kind of support. If we don't receive the correct support, we will come out deformed. The worst thing that can happen is that we're not allowed to suffer, mourn, rejoice, be angry, or hurt. When we don't have a positive support system, we end up like an obese butterfly, never able to reach our full potential because our burden is too heavy for our little wings to support.

We can't allow someone to enable us instead of giving us tough love, or pacify us instead of spanking us. No one wants to admire the process it takes to create a natural pearl, we just want to see the pearl. We don't want the pain, we just want the baby. Forget the hard work, give me the trophy. Keep the labor, give me the check. While we can't afford to have someone enable us or pacify us with shortcuts, we also can't allow someone to abuse us mentally, physically, or emotionally. The happy medium is assertiveness.

When you put all the components of a positive support system in a blender and mix it all together, it comes out smooth. Not in chunks, not runny, but smooth. Not passive, not aggressive, but assertive.

How did Nelson Mandela make it 27 years in prison? Positive Support System. How did Helen Keller make it through life deaf and blind? Positive Support System. Walt Disney persevered through 300 rejections from banks, Oprah was told she wasn't fit for TV, Thomas Edison tried over a 1,000 times to invent the light bulb, and the Wright Brothers suffered depression and family problems before inventing the airplane. Without the proper support, we would not have enjoyed the wonderful moments initiated by these products of positive support systems.

Do you have a positive support system? Appoint yourself as casting director and find people in your life to fulfill the roles of Cheerleader, TLC, Motivator, and ESPN.

The vision I have for my life is so big I cannot accomplish my goals and dreams by myself. I need a positive support system.

# WEDNESDAY

"Ask not what your country can do for you, but ask what you can do for your country."

John F. Kennedy

## BIB OR APRON?

At the time of this writing, I am an employee of Escambia District Schools. As mentioned in previous chapters, I am the head football coach at Escambia High School. There are a few millionaires who graduated from Escambia High School. Three were football players: Emmitt Smith, Trent Richardson, and Ahtyba Rubin. People often ask me if these gentlemen give money back to their school and community. My answer is always "yes" because they do. We actually had an alum who was not an athlete donate $10,000. He asked to remain anonymous. Thank you Mr. Brad Buhr. Oops. However, people only want to know if the athletes give back.

This question tells you the mind-set of some people. For some reason, it is human nature to try and find a flaw in people and point it out. After I confirm that our famous alumni do donate to our program, people usually want to know how much, and how often, or if they ever visit the school. Instead of answering, I ask them how often they give back or visit their high school. If they believe a millionaire should give 10% of his check to his alma mater, shouldn't they do the same? I have yet to meet a person who has asked that question who gives money to their high school.

We have a different set of standards for people we believe are above or beneath us. If we expect others to give back or serve, shouldn't we do the same? Are you a servant? Do you serve, or are you sitting in a high chair waiting to be served? We all should put on an apron and look for a way to serve. Great leaders are servant leaders. Leaders of great power are great at serving people. The question was asked: What do you do if you're the most powerful person in the room?

If you are the CEO, the mayor, the boss, the principal, the head coach, the pastor, the crew chief, the general, or the section leader, what do you do? There may come a time when you are the most powerful person in the room. What should you do with this power? Sit up straight?

Look important? Wear a shirt that says *I Am in Charge*? What do you do?

The fourth gospel of the New Testament is a narrative written by the apostle John. He says in John 13:3 that Jesus had all power. Then, in verse four, he says Jesus started the process of washing his followers' dirty feet.

The question: What do you do when you are the most powerful person in the room? Answer: You get on your knees and start washing feet.

Jesus was the greatest leader of all time. His form of leadership is known as servant leadership. Lead by serving. Apron, not bib. Custodian, not Principal. Flight attendant, not pilot. Water boy, not head coach. Private, not sergeant major.

During the height of his career, a reporter alleged that Muhammad Ali only gave back or participated in charitable events because he needed publicity. Ali agreed that he did need publicity for his fights, his books, and his appearances, but not for the charitable work he does. He said that if he was doing it for recognition, it was not a sincere gesture.

Almost thirty years later, in 1990, he proved that statement to be true. That year, he traveled to Iraq to sit down with Saddam Hussein to make a plea for peace. When Iraq invaded Kuwait, Hussein took a group of U.S. civilians hostage with plans to use them as shields to prohibit U.S. military strikes. Though Ali was in the beginning stages of Parkinsons disease and could not talk or walk very well, he risked his reputation, freedom, and safety to help people he didn't even know. The hostages were eventually set free due to Ali's brave efforts. Six weeks later, Operation Desert Storm attacked Iraq.

What if Ali would have said, it's none of my business. I don't know those people. I'll pray for them. What if he put on a bib instead of an apron? If he had, those hostages would have died.

My uncle served in the military, and he is currently in the reserves. He has worked through the school district and other agencies in an effort to find a young man to mentor. His own children are college graduates and are finding a way to contribute to society. Instead of taking the path of least resistance or complaining about the problems in our country, he has mentored a different young man every year for the past 22 years. People who don an apron believe that others have an intrinsic value. This belief prompts servant leaders to aide in the growth of others. To soften the soil, plant the seed, add the water, or provide the sunshine. Hillary Clinton said, "It takes a village to raise a child." Sometimes it takes a village of one to get things started.

The only reason many of us don't mentor is because we don't want to get outside our comfort zone. It is uncomfortable to help others, especially when they are different. Mentoring is one way to wear the apron. Another way is empathy.

Do you hurt when others hurt? Do you personalize the situation and ask yourself, *what if that was me or my son or my daughter?* When we empathize with others, it helps us make better decisions when we interact with them.

One of my greatest faults is my lack of compassion. I am not naturally compassionate. I am known to say things like, "Why are you crying? Tears don't move me." While I recognize the importance of having emotional balance, compassion doesn't come easy for me. When I'm hurt, I cry, and then I stop and keep it moving. My issue with empathy is that those who wallow in despair can seem weak and helpless. However, when it hits home for us, when we can identify with someone who is struggling, we often change our minds.

It is difficult to feel sorry for someone when their area of struggle is your area of strength. It is hard to relate, but if we are about serving, not being served, we must find a way to empathize.

A wise man once said: Those who humble themselves will be exalted. Those who exalt themselves will be humbled.

Bibs are for babies.

Are you wearing an apron or a bib?

# Thursday

"If what is true for you is for you, and what is true for me is true for me, what if my truth says your truth is a lie? Is it still true?"

Lecrae

## What is Truth?

If you asked 100 random people if they thought that they were a good person, most of them would say yes. Most of us believe we are good, moral, and decent people. I learned a lot about my own morals through studying ethics in college. Ethics, taught by Larry Justice, was one of my favorite courses at Northwestern State in Oklahoma. One day Mr. Justice gave us this test:

Question: It is time to elect a new world leader, and only your vote counts. Here are the facts about the three leading candidates.

Candidate A: Associates with crooked politicians, and consults with astrologists. He's had two mistresses. He also chain smokes and drinks 8 to 10 martinis a day.

Candidate B: He was kicked out of office twice, sleeps until noon, used opium in college, and drinks a quart of whiskey every evening.

Candidate C: He is a decorated war hero. He's a vegetarian, doesn't smoke, drinks an occasional beer, and has never cheated on his wife.

Which of these candidates would be your choice? Decide first, no peeking, then keep reading for the answer.

Candidate A is Franklin D. Roosevelt.
Candidate B is Winston Churchill.
Candidate C is Adolph Hitler.

Which of these candidates would be your choice?

All three of these men were considered good people by somebody. We all are good people. In our country we believe that child molesters and murders are bad and everyone else is negotiable. There are many people who don't take care of their children that are "good people." There are people who don't pay taxes, don't support our leaders, and break the law who are "good people."

The man who took care of my grandmother on her death bed is a wanted drug dealer who carries a gun without a permit. However, I could make a case for him as a "good person." There are people who lie, cheat, and steal on a regular basis and someone considers them "good."

In the above ethics exercise whom did you vote for?

Franklin D. Roosevelt, 32nd president of the United States
Winston Churchill, prime minister of the United Kingdom
Adolph Hitler, führer of Germany

Many of our assumptions of "good" are based on our limited knowl-edge of a person and our own self-evaluation. The same is true when it comes defining Truth.

How do we answer the tough questions of life?

While I was teaching about the dangers of alcohol, one of my students confessed that her parents allowed her to drink alcohol with the family on special occasions. This mother had a good job, wasn't an outcast, and was considered by all to be a "good" person. However, it is against the law to give minors alcohol. It is illegal for the young lady to con-sume alcohol. Many would condone this behavior with the justification that it only happens on special occasions. However, if I asked you if it were okay to break the law, most responsible people would say no, under no circumstances.

Another student told me that his parents allowed his girlfriend to sleep over, and she eventually moved in. He wanted to know why he should not have sex with her. He made some valid points. He said they were in love; he was going to marry her someday; she was his only girlfriend; and he would never hurt her. His question was this: *What is wrong with us being sexually active if that is what both of us want.* Good question. What do you think?

I have had students who have brought guns and knives to school for protection. I have known people who felt the need to have an abortion, and others who felt more comfortable dating someone of their same gender. I know people who feel there is nothing wrong with destroying property if the company is rich and has insurance as long as no one is physically hurt. Is this right? Who knows?

Lecrae Moore is a song writer. He wrote a song titled "Truth." In the song he says:

> It's just some folks say, "All truth is relative, it just depends on what you believe." You know, "hey man, ain't no way to know for sure who God is or what's really true." But that means you believe your own statement; that there's no way to know what's really true. You're saying that that statement is true. You're killing yourself. If what's true for you is true for you and what's true for me is true for me, what if my truth says yours is a lie? Is it still true?

He goes on to talk about secular humanism, which says that man is the source of all meaning and all purpose.

I use this to highlight the fact that most of us don't have a moral compass. We have no clue how to decide what is right and what is wrong. There is so much to consider, so many factors. The way I decide and the way I morally navigate through life is the Bible.

The Bible sucks sometimes. It's offensive. It's tough. It won't let me do whatever I want to do or go wherever I want to go. It won't allow me to watch what I want to watch or listen to what I want to listen to. However, it is my moral compass. Many people don't use the Bible in a literal sense. I don't have a problem with that. Some ministers and Christians force their beliefs on others. Not me, I'm different. I believe people should do whatever they want, but they shouldn't complain about the consequence of their actions. However, if the way you deal with life is not working for you, try Jesus. You've tried everything else. Try Jesus. If you want to know what that looks like, I would love to tell you about it.

If I had a million dollars, you would probably want to know how I earned it. I'm a nice guy, so I would tell you. If I won five state championships as a coach, you would probably want to know how we did it, and I would share. When I meet someone who has been married for more than twenty-five years, I ask them how they did it. Whenever I meet successful people, I try to pick their brains.

There are things in the Bible that I do not understand, and other things that I do not agree with. However, I made a decision to use it as the guide for my life. So whenever a tough situation comes up, I can go to the Bible for the answer. If I decided to make a decision that is contrary to what the Bible teaches, I know that I am wrong. I don't have to ask myself if my behavior or action is right or wrong, I will know that I made a decision to do the wrong thing.

I believe the problem is that we are not sure if we are right or wrong. We often use our feelings and advice from our unqualified friends to make decisions. This often leads us down the road of uncertainty. We end up doing what feels right, or what seems right. With the Bible as my moral compass, I have no problem knowing what is right or wrong.

A compass is a map. How am I to know what to do and where to go? I need help. I depend on my faith. 100%.

# FRIDAY

"It's hard to be humble, when you're as great as I am."

Muhammad Ali

## SPORTS: POSITIVES AND NEGATIVES

I am a not a big sports fan, but I am a big fan of sports. I don't have a favorite team or favorite player. However, I enjoy watching sports on television or listening on the radio. I am also a history buff. I enjoy documentaries on historical events. My Christmas gift from my wife the past two years has been ESPN's *30 for 30* series. We have them all recorded on DVR, and I have the DVD's. It is the best of both worlds-historical documentaries on different sports stories. I love to watch the documentaries because they are always stories about the positives and negatives in sports. These historical films teach me something every time I watch them.

Sports may be our greatest teacher. Imagine a young girl with low self-esteem playing basketball. One day she throws up a lucky shot to win the game. Instantly, her self-esteem rises and the effects could last forever. Imagine a teenage boy who is arrogant and cocky guarding the opposing team's best player. Down by one point with 15 seconds re-maining, the young man steals the ball and heads down the court while the last seconds tick by. He has a wide open lay-up for the win, but he misses the shot, causing his team to lose. He is instantly humbled.

Think about the first deer you shot, the first fish you caught, the first time you ran a 5k, or dunked a basketball. Imagine bowling the perfect game or hitting a hole in one in golf. What could top that feeling? When Tom Brady became the youngest quarterback ever to win three Super Bowls they asked him what he would do next. He said, "Win another Super Bowl."

We will never be satisfied. If we are fortunate enough to win, we want to win some more. We're feeding a monster. This can be a negative side of sports. Vince Lombardi, one of the greatest football coaches of all time, said, "Gentlemen, we will chase perfection, and we will chase it relentlessly, knowing all the while we can never attain it. But along the way, we shall catch excellence."

The problem comes when we forget that perfection is not attainable. The negative side of sports is winning at all costs. Cutting corners and cheating to gain an edge. It happens in little league, high school, college, and the pros. Why? Why cheat? There are so many reasons to cheat. You cheat to keep up with your opponents, to win, to gain more money, prestige, or fame. You cheat in order to get the same feeling you had when you won that first championship or shot that deer, caught that fish, or ran that 5k. The feeling cannot be duplicated; you can't replicate it. However, we chase it like we are Florence Griffin Joyner or Jessie Owens, Marian Jones or Ben Johnson.

I know high school football coaches who make over one hundred thousand dollars a year. The top college football and basketball coaches make well over three million dollars a year. If you made this kind of money for the work you do, wouldn't you be tempted to turn your head when someone is flirting with the line of dishonesty in an effort to help you keep your job?

Still, there is a feeling that comes with winning that money can't buy. It is the feeling of knowing that you are the best in the room, and the fact that everyone else knows it too makes you feel good. You don't have to say anything. They know it. While this is a great feeling, you must be careful, or the new stride you have in your walk can lead you directly to arrogance.

Study any sports program, and you can see the positives and negatives of sports. I've seen high school students play their hearts out and never graduate from high school. I have known players who have won championships but lose in every other area of life. Coaches who are great fathers to everyone else's children, but don't have time for their own children.

On the other hand, I have also seen sports bring families closer together. It is awesome to watch father and daughter throwing the softball in the yard, or mother and son shooting hoops in the driveway. If you are involved with travel ball, you see families come together to root for their athlete. You experience many different emotions together. One minute you are screaming for joy, the next minute you're screaming at the referee. One summer you cry because your athlete was injured- out for the rest of the season, and the next summer you cry tears of joy because they won the championship. You love the coach today, but only tolerate her tomorrow. You go out to eat together, you bond, you fight, you smile, you worry, you argue, and the very next day you hug.

The best thing that can happen from participating in sports is learning life lessons. You will learn traits like hard work, discipline, teamwork, perseverance, and how to handle both success and failure. The benefit of exercise through sports is also significant. Tennis and golf players can play their sports well into their senior years. These, along with walking, are sporting activities one can use for life.

The worst thing that can happen from participating in sports is that one can lose focus on why they are playing in the first place. Have you ever seen an irate parent or coach at a little league game? This usually happens when the adult has lost focus. Have you ever heard of an athlete cheating? This usually happens when the athlete has lost focus. Most people started playing sports because they wanted to have fun. It seems like we have gotten away from that in some aspects.

What role do sports play in your life? Are you a big college football or college basketball fan? Do you have a child or grandchild that plays sports? Do you golf or walk, run or play tennis? Do you get together with friends to play basketball or volleyball? I hope the purpose for your participation is fun. Life is too short to settle for good. Make it a great experience.

How can you do from good to great in the area of sports?

# WEEKEND APPLICATION

The goal is to pick two of the five items we discussed this week and make an effort to go from good to great in that area. After deciding which two you want to focus on, formulate a plan of action. Then ask yourself, *What am I going to each day to accomplish my goal?* Be sure to chart your progress and reward yourself periodically.

## Monday- Know Your Role

Is it hard for you to stay in your lane? Is it hard for you to mind your own business? I know it is hard to watch someone mess up a situation that you could make better. However, we all have an assignment, a role, a job, a position. I challenge you to Do *Your* Job.

## Tuesday- Positive Support System

Who's got your back? If you don't have supportive friends in your circle, you need to change that immediately. Who motivates you? Who shows you tough love? Who cheers for you? Who lends an ear to you when you're most vulnerable?

## Wednesday- Bib or Apron

Do you have your hand out? Are you looking for a hand out? Is it time for you to start growing up and serving instead of being served? Are you giving of your time and money? Do you volunteer, mentor, or write a check in support of others?

## Thursday- What is Truth?

Where do you stand on abortion? Homosexuality? Monogamy? Co-habitating? Marijuana? The death penalty? If a rude and disrespectful convicted child molester or murderer leaves their wallet on the city bus with $500 in it, do you return it? How you decide what to do? Who's your guide?

## Friday-Sports the Positive and Negative

How can you use sports to take your life from good to great?

# TRANSFORMING YOUR LIFE FROM GOOD TO GREAT

## DAILY NUGGETS OF WISDOM

# WEEK THREE

# MONDAY

"The quality, not the longevity, of one's life is what is important."

Martin Luther King, Jr.

## QUALITY OR QUANTITY

If I sat in a rocking chair, it would move back and forth as long as I sat in it and rocked. I could sit there and rock for five hours and not go anywhere. Movement and progress are not same. Just because there is activity does not mean there is progress. In business, in education, and in life, we tend to think that bigger is better, and that *more* is more meaningful.

We assume the church with the most people is the better church, that the library with the most books has the best books, that the grocery store with the most aisles has the better groceries. However, when you think about it, the better the quality is, the less available the product usually is. High quality food is hard to find, but fast food is on every corner. High quality cars are almost impossible to find, while regular cars are easy to come by. When it comes to products, we understand this principal; but, for some reason, when it comes to our everyday lives, we still think more is better.

It is very possible to get a quality education at most universities. I believe that when it comes to education, you get out what you put in. Nonetheless, most students would rather go to a big college than a small college. Most performers want a big audience, regardless of the impact of their entertainment.

In the social media driven world in which we live, many people are chasing their 15 minutes of fame. Some quality poets, actors, magicians, and athletes can get caught up in fame seeking and neglect their original purpose.

Do you have a purpose or mission statement for your life, your business, or your family? This statement could help you keep the main thing the main thing. Why do you do what you do? How did you get where you are? How will you get where you're going?

While starring as Troy Maxson in the August Wilson play *Fences,* Academy Award-winning actor Denzel Washington revealed that he prefers acting on stage over acting on screen. In the interview with the *New York Times* and *City Television,* he quoted *The Great Debaters,* a film which he himself directed, "We do what we have to do so we can do what we want to do." He went on to say that movies pay the bills, but while he enjoys his work, acting on stage is what he enjoys more. He enjoys the true art of acting, the energy of the audience, the opportunity to add depth to the character night after night.

Denzel makes twenty million dollars a movie, yet he gets more joy out of acting on stage. He admits that he enjoys the quality of acting in theater over the quantity or the big time of traditional movies. He said sometimes characters in film get watered down, the budgets get bigger, and sometimes the depth of the character is lost.

Have you lost something? Have you lost your hunger? Why did you start teaching? What made you put that guitar down? Why did you give up cooking? Why did you pick up that camera? Why did you start that business? Have you lost the passion? Have you lost sight of why you started down this path in the first place?

Sometimes life happens, and we forget why we are where we are. You have to get that fire back. You have to rekindle that flame. Don't worry about what others think. Don't worry about making it big. Return to your roots. Get that old feeling back.

I challenge you to find that one thing that gave you goose bumps, the thing that made your heart beat fast. What is it you love to do? Find a way to choose quality over quantity in different areas of life.

Quality is not always popular. Quantity is. Be true to yourself. Life is too short to just be good. Be great. Don't just survive. Thrive.

# TUESDAY

"Those things that hurt, instruct."

Benjamin Franklin

## THE KEY INGREDIENT TO SUCCESS

Failure is the key to success. However, failing forward is an art form predicated on careful planning and risk management. Michael Jordan, arguably the best basketball player ever, said, "I have missed more than 9,000 shots in my career. I have lost almost 300 games. On 26 occasions I have been entrusted to take the game winning shot, and I missed. I have failed over and over and over again in my life. And that is why I succeed."

Like Michael Jordan, I have had my share of failures. In high school, I was rated a three star football player by *Forrest Davis Recruiting,* a high school recruiting magazine. According to their assessment of my athletic ability, I would start at wide receiver for a division one college as a junior and senior. According to the NCAA eligibility requirements, I needed to make a 21 on the ACT because my core grade point average was below a 2.5. Although my grades had improved tremendously my junior and senior years, they were not enough to overturn my lack of effort my first two years in high school.

Every week, I would receive letters from division one schools. Some were handwritten by the head football coach, while others sent two letters per day. All I had to do was make a 21 on the college entrance exam, the ACT. I made a 17 the first time. The second time I took the test, I had a feeling I would do much better. I checked the mail every day, and I had already planned on running around the block screaming at the top of my lungs once I received news that I made the appropriate score.

The day finally came. I opened mailbox, and there it was. With my heart beating fast, palms sweaty from adrenaline, I opened the envelope. 17. My score was a 17, again. I was not good enough for a college to wait on me, and it was too late to take the test again because there were so many equally talented players that were qualified.

I failed.

I did, however, find a college, and I enjoyed four great years of football. Once I graduated from college, I had to figure out what I would do for a career. I hired an agent, and he submitted my name into the NFL Europe draft. I never received a call. He set up a tryout with the Canadian Football League, but it was rained out twice and the coach stop returning my calls. I eventually played for three different teams in the Arena Football League, the indoor professional league, and had a great time. My goal was to play in the NFL.

I failed.

As I continued to search for a career, I decided to pursue an opportunity as an entertainer. I sent my video host tape (actual VHS tape) to MTV and BET. I heard nothing. I was an award winning college disc jockey and radio host, so I sent my award winning tape (actual cassette) to KKDA- K104 in Dallas, Texas; WBLX in Mobile, Alabama; and two radio stations in my home town of Panama City. Crickets....I heard nothing but crickets. I did spend time working at WDKX in Rochester, New York, and two years as a DJ on Disney Cruise Line.

My goal was to work for MTV or BET. I failed.

While working on the cruise line, my high school football coach called me about a teaching and coaching position at the high school. After coaching for a few years, I realized I wanted to become a head coach. I worked as head coach of track, basketball, weightlifting, and volleyball, but I really wanted to try my hand as a head football coach.

The first thing I did was talk to my principal about someday applying for the head football coaching position at my high school alma mater; he talked to me like I was 15 years old and laughed. I then applied for several head coaching positions. White noise. Nothing. No one called. No one acknowledge my interest. I finally got an interview at a school whose football team never wins. They told me that I was great in the interview, but they were going in a different direction. They actually offered me a position on the new coaches' staff. I declined.

Why is failure so important? The reason failure is important is that we learn the most from failure. It is difficult to learn from success. If everyone is telling you how great you are, there is no time to reflect on mistakes or errors. The end result is what we wanted, so we turn our eyes away from the problems that occurred along the way. Another reason failure is important is because you find out who you really are when you fail. When we are squeezed, who we really are becomes manifest.

I experienced professional failure before I got in the door as a professional. On my quest to become a teacher and head football coach, I signed up to take the teacher certification exam. I needed a score of 200 in order to pass the subject area exam. I scored above 194 five times without reaching 200.

There are several parts to the test. The General Knowledge section is made up of four parts: math, reading, essay, and reading language skills. I passed all but the math portion the first time I took the General Knowledge Test. The next test is a test of pedagogy and professional practices called the Professional Education Test. I passed this test on the first try because through practice tests I learned what type of answer they were looking for. The final test is the subject area test. I decided to pick the easiest subject I had in school: physical education. I did not study for the test, and on my first attempt I scored a 174, I needed a 200.

Why did I fail the test so many times? Am I not smart? Was it too difficult? Is it because I was not an education major? Was it because I am not a good test taker?

In all, I failed to pass the Florida Teacher Certification Exam twelve times. I had failed, again. Or did I? Because I learned from my mistakes, I did eventually pass all the portions of the certification test. Just as all of my wife's pound cakes don't turn out perfectly, my failures have helped me more than any success.

There are ways to prevent failure or better your chances for success. When I speak at high schools, I always notice the senior class is the smallest and the freshmen class is the largest. What happens to students between ninth and twelfth grades? They drop out. In America, over 7,000 student drop out of high school every day. These young people don't realize that failure is the key ingredient to success. If you fall, get back up. If you fail, try again. The only surefire way to avoid failure is to not try, which makes you failure.

Failure is only failure if you don't learn from it and achieve something. There are ten basic factors that prevent us from achieving after a failure:

- Poor organizational skills

- Bad teammates

- Poor planning

- Unrealistic goals

- Poor work ethic

- Not seeking wise counsel

- Lack of motivation

- No available resources

- Lack of ability

- Poor timing

Many of these factors we can control. A wise man once said, "I can't worry about those things which I cannot control." In education, the uncontrollable variable is parents. In business, it is the economy. When I worked on the cruise ship, it was the weather. There are things we can control and there are things we cannot. A successful person will embrace failure as part of the equation for success.

In 1983, head basketball coach at North Carolina State, Jim Valvano was leading the team least likely to win the NCAA National Basketball Championship. Nevertheless, they won the championship! He is known for saying, "Don't give up. Don't ever give up."

# WEDNESDAY

"Lazy hands make a man poor, but diligent hands bring wealth."

Proverbs 10:4

## FINANCES

As a young boy, I would earn money by mowing grass. My first steady job was working through the Job Training Partnership Act of 1982. This was a law signed by President Ronald Regan. In 1998, under President Bill Clinton, the act was repealed, though many of its provisions were absorbed by the new Workforce Investment Act. It was through this federal aid program that I worked at the Boys Club during the summer of 1992. Minimum wage was $4.25 an hour, and that was my salary. I worked eight hours a day, five days a week, for five hundred dollars a month after taxes.

I remember receiving my first check. I was so happy. I had already decided what to spend my money on. Air Jordan shoes $130.00; football, baseball, and basketball cards $100.00; a milkshake from Gardner's Drug every day $1.15 per day for 5 days a week; and Chicago Bulls hat and shirt $50.00. I don't recall the other items on my list, but I do remember that I had every penny spent. I asked my dad to cash my check for me at his bank and bring me back the money. He had something else in mind.

He sat down while I stood and listened to him talk for almost an hour on managing money. I was fourteen-years-old and was trying to figure out what made him think he was a financial guru. To say we lived a modest lifestyle would be an over-estimation of our circumstances, but we always had food, shelter, and transportation. If you were a fly on the wall, though, you would think my dad was Joe Granville or some economics expert. It was like he had just watched the Suze Orman show or read one of Dave Ramsey's books. However, Suze Orman did not go on the air until 2002, and while Dave Ramsey had just completed his first book *Financial Peace,* my dad didn't have a copy of it. I didn't have a choice, so I stood there and listened.

He told me that I was going to pay ten percent of my paycheck to the church in the form of a tithe and ten percent to myself as savings. This sounded like the dumbest thing I had ever heard in my life. First of all, the church didn't need my money, and why would I pay myself ten percent? The church looked fine to me, and the pastor had more suits than we had pews. I had already decided to pay myself one hundred percent, since I earned one hundred percent of the money. He also talked about paying bills on time and not borrowing money if I could help it. I contemplated quitting the job, especially if I had to pay the church and myself every time I got a pay check. I am glad I did not.

I would be lying if I told you that I had mastered every nugget in this book. The nugget in which I am most deficient is probably this one - finances. I do, however, believe God has placed people in my life to keep me afloat financially because of my faithfulness as a young person in paying my tithe or paying the church. My dad proved to be on to something.

Suze Orman has ten tips for a fresh financial start and Dave Ramsey has seven baby steps to financial peace. I guarantee these two financial gurus have forgotten more about financial freedom than I know. However, the advice my father gave me is great advice.

If you are a person of faith the first thing you need to do when you get your check is pay ten percent to your church. The Bible says in Malachi 3:8 *Will a mere mortal rob God? Yet you rob me. "But you ask, 'How are we robbing you?' In tithes and offerings."*

I believe it is the job of the people who say they believe in God to keep the church afloat financially if they believe in what the church is doing. If the people who say they believe in God won't support the church, who will?

If you do not believe in paying tithe, you should give ten percent to your favorite charity. The next ten percent should go in a bank account that will not be touched. These two principals can help you do a better job of managing your money. I know it can be difficult.

In 2003, my wife and I sold our first house and used the money to get out of debt. We then bought a house and thought that we would be financially stable for a long time. After living in the house for less than a year, we moved to another city to take a different job. We never sold the home. We paid rent at one home and mortgage on the one we were trying to sell for a total of $3,000.00 a month for two years. It wiped us out, and put us back in the hole. When you add the cost of two small children in day care, two automobile payments, student loans, cell phones, cable, groceries, lights, water, etc., you can see how we got far behind.

My wife and I were bringing home teacher salaries, and I was trying to get my speaking and writing business off the ground. Ultimately, I briefly left the education field to work full-time in an athletic ministry where I would have to raise my own salary. Not even a year into my job with the Fellowship of Christian Athletes, I left to take a job which paid half my previous two salaries to pursue my dream of becoming a head football coach. I actually went three months without a salary at all.

Through all of this, I remained faithful in paying my tithe and paying myself. Common sense tells us to not buy things we can't afford, and to live within our means. Why would you buy a new car when the one you have works fine? Why get a new cell phone for $200.00 dollars if the one you have works well. We often lack discipline, and we have to fight the urge to keep up with the Joneses.

I have a long way to go before I can facilitate a workshop on financial freedom; however, taking that twenty percent off the top has helped me tremendously.

What will you do to go from good to great financially?

# Thursday

"Positive thinking will let you do everything better than negative thinking will."
Zig Ziglar

## Glass Half–Full

When I go to Chick-fil-A, I look forward to hearing the workers say "my pleasure." I spent some time with an operator of a Chick-fil-A in Georgia named Justin. I was scheduled to speak with his employees in a professional development session. The speaking engagement never materialized, but we hung out a few times and shared a few laughs.

He impressed me with his ability to hire the right people and his knowledge and perspective on different issues. We lived in the same neighborhood and had the same values. Although he is a great husband and father, I never heard him use the phrase "my pleasure" at home. He would say thank you, I'm sorry, excuse me, and yes ma'am to his wife (because he was afraid of her.) However, he never said "my pleasure".

There was one boy who worked for Justin who thought that he was a thug. When I saw the young man at school, I would tease him saying, "Yeah, you're tough now, but from 4:00 to close you have your pants pulled up, a smile on your face, and you say my pleasure. Say it, say it." He would get upset with me. When I went into Chick-fil-A, I would ask for him and would purposely say, "Thank you."

He would always respond, "My pleasure."

The founder of Chick-fil-A, Truett Cathy had a great vision for fast food and the chicken sandwich. It appears that Chick-fil-A employees don't have bad days. It seems as if they never wake up on the wrong side of the bed. If you didn't know any better, you would think they all enjoy their lives and jobs, and that they enjoy serving customers. No matter how bad things seem, they approach each encounter as if the glass is half full, not half empty.

You can look at any situation both ways. You can either say the glass is half full or that the glass is half empty. When I worked for Disney, the weather report would be 30% chance of sunshine instead of 70% chance of rain. It's all about perspective.

In 2008, I took a job working in full time sports ministry for the Fellowship of Christian Athletes (FCA). In October of that year, I flew to Kansas City Missouri for a week-long training. While I was, there I met another former coach who had a great perspective on life named Mark Tidwell.

Mark and I have similar personalities, and we love God and sports. We made fun of all the different people at the training and clowned on each other quite a bit. Once I left Missouri and returned to my South Georgia home, I wondered if I would ever see any of those people again.

As time has passed, I have spent time with several people whom I met for the first time during that great autumn week. In 2012, my wife and I spent a week in St. Simons, Georgia, at the Epworth camp for an FCA Coaches Camp. Lo and behold, who was there passing out t-shirts with his beautiful wife, Lee? Yep, my buddy Mark.

Mark and I picked up where we left off and commenced to clowning and holding up the line. Later in the week, Mark asked me to speak. I initially declined, because my intent was to be refreshed during the week by being poured into by the different activities and speakers. However, he was persistent, and I agreed to speak on Thursday, the last night of camp.

I am a confident speaker. I pray, prepare, and pitch. I do get nervous, but I feel good about my God given ability to keep people's attention and motivate them through knowledge, stories, laughter, and strategies. People often say that I'm a hard act to follow, but I smile and do my best to remain humble.

On the night before I was to speak to the 200 plus coaches and their wives, Mark spoke. Mark is handsome, smart, charismatic, and funny. I knew he would do a great job of letting God use him. Plus, it's not a contest; we're all on the same team.

Mark started by telling jokes and making fun of those in the room and then he shared his testimony:

*I'll never forget the words I heard on March 16, 2009. I was in a doctor's office, and he entered the room and said, "Mr. Tidwell, we found the problem and that problem is colon cancer and we need to take care of it as soon as possible." At that moment, my life as I knew it changed. Four days later, I entered the hospital and had the cancer removed. The doctors were very positive and thought they got everything, and we thought we would move on and this would be a speed bump. Three months later when I came back for scans, the news wasn't so good. Our oncologist entered the room this time. We could tell by the look on her face and her body language that the news was not as positive as we would have hoped for. She says, "Mark, I hate to tell you this but the cancer has metastasized and now you've developed stage four liver cancer." A few weeks later, I entered the hospital once again and had tumors from my liver removed, and we continued to progress from that point till recovery. Unfortunately, I had complications a few months later and had to go back again and have some more surgery done. In March 2010, we got the next news that the cancer had come back to the liver, so we started seeking additional input and consultation. We flew to the Mayo Clinic in Minnesota and they confirmed the cancer was there in the liver.*

The room was dead silent. The entire week, he had been the most energetic person there, with a smile on his face and an attitude of gratitude. If he would not have shared the fact that he was dying, we would have never known. He decided to live a life with a glass-half-full mentality.

What about you?

In October 2011, my cousin was arrested and later sentenced to life in prison. I visit him and write him often, but not often enough. He is always upbeat, optimistic, and has a smile on his face. Every time I go to see him, I am amazed at his demeanor and posture. How can he be facing life in prison when he is only twenty-five years old? When he was married for one week when he was arrested? He faces his situation with optimism. He says that there is no evidence against him and that he will get out one day.

What about you?

This is why I say life is good. If you don't believe your life is good, compare your life to Mark or to my cousin. The both are facing a life sentence and they believe their lives are good. Why are we complaining? Why are we finding ways to gripe? Why can't we see the glass as half-full instead of half-empty?

# FRIDAY

"Winning is not a sometime thing, it's an all the time thing."

Vince Lombardi

## WINNING IS IMPORTANT

In coaching and in life, winning is important. Winners are respected. They just are. Consistent winners are admired and praised, but those who win the big one have the greatest stage. Is Miami Heat head coach Erik Spoelstra a better coach than retired NBA coach Jerry Sloan? Are Jon Gruden and John Madden better coaches Marty Schottenheimer or Marv Levy? Does the teacher who has no credentials have as much influence as the teacher-of-the-year who always meets adequate yearly progress and is national-board-certified? Does the salesman of the year get an opportunity to talk at the annual banquet, or the guy who sold the least? Who influences the country the most, for good or bad, Barack Obama or Mitt Romney? Political opinions aside, the more influential person is President Obama. Why? Because he won. When talking about influence, the perception is that winning is important, but winning the big one is most important.

King David is not well-known for being anointed king at a young age, or for his gift of music, or even for his failure as a husband and father. He is most known for his greatest failures and greatest victories. David defeating Goliath is the greatest upset of all time. The 1980 USA hockey team defeating the Soviet Union in the Olympics, or James Buster Douglas's 1990 defeat of Mike Tyson in Tokyo, have nothing on David defeating Goliath. Tyler Perry's rags to riches story is great because he won big, therefore he has great influence.  Like these examples, King David defeating Goliath changed his status and his range of influence.

In 1999, I played football for Northwestern Oklahoma State University, a small NAIA school in Alva, Oklahoma. The school has since moved up to NCAA Division II and competes in the Great American Conference. The 1999 team is the *winningest* team in school history, and is the only team from NWOSU to win a National Championship in any sport. Two of the teams that followed us were runners- up, and there has been great success at our school in other areas, including the NWOSU basketball team beating Baylor in 1995.

Winning the big one on our tiny level, changed lives. I could write a book on the trickledown effect of that championship season (and I will one day.) Two weeks after our win, our head football coach Tim Albin was hired by the University of Nebraska. Within two years, seven players from that team (Patrick Crayton, Ron Moore, Lynn Scott, Brandon Christiansen, Isaac Harvin, Dustin Loveless, and Preston Hartfield) played in an NFL game.

As a coach or player, striving to win a game or striving to win the big one is a mistake. The goal must be to get better every day and embrace the process. This will ensure victory in other areas. Winning is not the most important outcome; however, it is very important.

As a coach, I try to stay focused on the fundamentals. The way I do this is by teaching the core values of the FCA: Integrity, Serving, Teamwork, and Excellence. We try to make an impact in the community and in the lives of the each player. A friend named Coach Price once told a player to not be ok with being ok.

We stress those principles. Seize the Day, *Carpe Diem*. You get out what you put in. If it were easy, everyone would do it. Don't be average.

We repeat all these clichés. We have a proven method of improving grades and test scores. We work hard in our strength and conditioning program. I have studied great coaches that I admire such as John Wooden, Bobby Bowden, Tony Dungy, Tom Osborne and Mark Richt. I have read their books, and have met a couple of them in person and picked their brains. But, ultimately, none of this preparation matters if we don't win.

If we don't win, we lose the influence to make a difference. If we don't win, we won't have a team to take to FCA Camp. We won't have a group of athletes to read to the elementary students. We won't have to reserve buses to take them on a college tour, or ask church members to donate ties for them to wear and learn how to tie.

Just like you need a license to drive, a degree to teach, and a whistle to coach, you need to win to have influence. You can drive without a license, and teach without a degree. You can even coach without a whistle; I've seen it done. However, you lose creditability, influence, and effectiveness when you don't have the right tools or credentials.

After working in six school districts and having more than 10 principals and six superintendents, I think I have learned what it takes to have a successful sports program. Athletes. If you don't have athletes, you won't win. You can have a great administration, great facilities, make a lot of money, have a great booster club, and phenomenal assistants. Still, you will not win without athletes. Nick Saban is considered one of the greatest football coaches of all time, yet he did not win a single national championship at Michigan State. On the other hand, he won multiple championships at Alabama, in part, because he had superior athletes.

Whenever someone says that it's only a game, they have identified themselves as only a fan. If you are a high school, college, or professional coach, your success is usually measured by wins and losses. Coach Bobby Bowden was asked if character, discipline, duty and honor were the most important things in college football. He responded by saying that if those qualities were truly the most important things in college football, the service academies would be ranked near the top every year. He believed that 80,000 people came to see his football team win, not study or be good citizens.

Despite this practical outlook, Coach Bowden was able to use his influence to make his players better men because he won. I know several former players who were blessed to play for Coach Bowden, and they all say he helped them become winners in life. Coaches should create winning moments for their players. On and off the field, catch them doing good things. Brag on their good grades, and good behavior. Likewise, we should all encourage young people in this manner. Whatever gets praised, gets repeated, good or bad.

Many don't know that King David's best friend was King Saul's son Jonathan, or that David had seven wives, or that one of his sons tried to kill him several times. Many don't know that the wisest man to ever live was David's son Solomon. There is so much we don't know about David, but everyone knows that David defeated Goliath.

John Wooden said he coached the same way in 1948, when he first took the job at UCLA, as he did 1975 when he retired. He won the first of ten national championships during the 1963-1964 season after being there for fifteen years. What happened? What took them from knocking on the door of championships to knocking the door down? I am sure there were many factors in their dominance, but one factor for sure was the talent of superstars Lewis Alcindor and Bill Walton. One thing that happened is that he coached some of the greatest basketball players in the school's history. His greatest tool was the belief in his system and ability; when superior play was added to this equation, the championships rolled in. He won ten national championships. That is more than anyone in any sport, and one reason he is considered one of the most influential coaches ever to coach. He has the most big-wins and he is most influential. See how that works.

Win. Find a way to win.

# WEEKEND APPLICATION

The goal is to pick two of the five items we discussed this week and make an effort to go from good to great in that area. After deciding which two you want to focus on, formulate a plan of action. Then ask yourself *What am I going to do each day to accomplish my goal*? Be sure to chart your progress and reward yourself periodically.

## Monday- Quality or Quantity

The Titanic sank because the most important part of the iceberg was below the water. The captain of the ship saw the small peak above the water, but the big part of the iceberg is what sank the ship. The most important part of us is the part that no one sees. Are you more concerned with your actual life or what it looks like? Reality or image? Quality or quantity?

## Tuesday- The Key to Success

Failure. Are you ready to embrace failure? "You miss 100% of the shots you don't take," said Wayne Gretzky, the greatest scorer in NHL history. Don't be afraid to fail. Go for it!

## Wednesday- Finances

Do you have a budget? Do you spend more than you make? Do you save? Do you give to nonprofit organizations? I try to pay my church 10% and myself 10%. This works for me.

## Thursday- Glass half full

Is it 30% chance of sunshine or 70% chance of rain? Is the glass half empty or half full? What is your perspective? How are you looking at the situation?

## Friday-Winning is Important

How do you know the names Mary Lou Retton and Gabbie Douglas? Do you follow gymnastics? No, you know their names because they are winners. Big Winners have big influence. Win Big.

# Transforming Your Life from Good to Great:

# Daily Nuggets of Wisdom

THE WILLIE SPEARS EXPERIENCE

# WEEK FOUR

# MONDAY

"Parents can only give good advice or put them on the right paths, but the final forming of a person's character lies in their own hands."

Anne Frank

## WHAT DON'T YOU WANT TO BE WHEN YOU GROW UP?

"What do you want to be when you grow up?" is a very common question asked of young people. In my experience with this question, the answers I get are very similar. Most young people want to be rich, famous, or have an occupation that does not take much effort. Some young people don't associate education with having a job as an entertainer or professional athlete. Therefore, the young man who has dreams of the NBA may not value education because he does not think he needs an education to accomplish his goal.

Our youth have goals based on false information. For some reason, their role models seldom talk about their intellect. Although Adam Levine, Beyonce, Jay-Z, Lebron James, and Lady Gaga are very smart, young people don't believe their success is synonymous with being a good student. It scares me that our youth look up to and admire people they really don't know. I wish they would find someone they could touch and see every day to emulate. In their ignorance, many of them have subconsciously said "I don't need school to become the next Lil Wayne, or Justin Bieber." Young people get a glimpse of the life of a celebrity and oftentimes try to make those four hours they see them on the television their twenty-four hour reality.

During the summer of 2003, I was asked by a nonprofit organization to work with a group of troubled young people. These were young people who lived in a low income housing development where many of their relatives were involved in crime. At any given time, as many as twenty-five percent of the inhabitants of this housing project were in the criminal justice system- in jail or prison, on parole or probation. These students were between the ages of 9-17, and only two of the forty had passed the state standardized test. One sixteen-year-old read at a second-grade level.

I was asked to help these young people overcome their circumstances. We took part in many team building exercises including a co-ed basketball team. We took field trips, and I did my best to place role models in front of them. I solicited the help of firemen, policemen, politicians, teachers, and other blue and white collar workers, in an effort to show them real people who have made good decisions.

Hypocritically, I tried to keep athletes and entertainers away from them. When I asked them what they wanted to be when they grew up almost all of them duplicated the answers I so often receive *rapper, singer, athlete.*

There was a young man named Isaac who had played high school football nearby and was an extra in one of the Superman movies. He had graduated from the University of Central Florida, and I thought he would make a great speaker.

Most people who speak to a group of this demographic start out by telling the audience a little about themselves, or they start off with a joke. Isaac started off by engaging the audience with a question. He asked them not what they wanted to be when they grew up, but what they didn't want to be when they grew up.  The answers were amazing. It opened up a discussion that instantly caused the young people to think cognitively and think outside the box. They took steps toward having a paradigm shift. They were forced to admit that the circumstances in which they found themselves in were not where they wanted to remain.

The answers: I don't want to be a drug dealer, I don't want to be in jail, I don't want to be dead, I don't want to be the daddy to a bunch of kids, I don't want to be somebody's baby-mamma, I don't want to be broke.

This dialogue was the catalyst for many conversations resulting in positive decision making projects.

One day, I gave them a lecture about the importance of education. I was on my soapbox. I told them if they wanted to have a good life, if they wanted to "be somebody" they would need an education. I continued, "A nice house, nice car, a nice life, requires an education and/or hard work."

A short, chunky girl with orange Cheetos dust on each finger raised her hand. I called on her immediately because this was an improvement from the screaming out of answers that I had experienced in previous meetings. She began to describe her lifestyle, "We live in a nice apartment, my momma has a car better than yours, we have cabinets and a refrigerator full of food, and my momma sits at home and watch the stories every day." The young lady was absolutely right, and this is what she wanted to do with her life. She did not see a problem with draining from society's resources and not giving back. The reason? Because her mother is the person from whom she learned her first values. This is an element we can't control.

However, we can encourage young people and help them to avoid becoming what they don't want to be. Many of them don't realize the military or community college both offer great opportunities for young people. Community colleges offer programs such as nursing, auto mechanics, computer technology, culinary arts, as well as training programs for dental hygienists, emergency medical technicians, and physical therapy assistants. Learning these skills can lead to jobs that offer good financial opportunities along with medical benefits.

*What don't you want to be?* The best answer to this question is this. I don't want to be lazy.

What don't you want to be?

# TUESDAY

"You can't make decisions based on fear and the possibility of what might happen."

Michelle Obama

## DECISION MAKING

Making decisions can prove difficult. For young people ages 16-25, it can prove very difficult. Who do I hang out with? Do I wear this or that? Do I join the band, or a club, or the team, or a gang? Do I smoke or not smoke, drink or not drink? Do I have sex now or wait? Do I get piercings, or tattoos, or both? Do I go to the military or college? Which branch of the military? Which college? Who do I marry? Am I Democrat or Republican? Protestant or Catholic? Baptist or Methodist?

There is no science to making these decisions. My dad used to tell me to chew up the meat and spit out the bones. In other words, take what I can from a situation and discard the rest. With that said, I am going to share how I make decisions. I have had to make some tough ones over the years. The biggest ones have come in my career. I started coaching in 2002. I have changed jobs nine times since then, and I had to make some very tough choices along the way. I started speaking professionally in 2006, and have had to make several tough decisions in this area as well.

Statistics suggest picking a spouse and a career are two of the toughest decisions people make. Almost half of marriages end in divorce, and over 70% of people work outside their degree field. This means that most people are making the wrong decisions.

I chose my wife based on practical principles, not emotions. We definitely love one another, but when I thought she may be the one, falling in love was not on the list. I wanted a smart woman with a job, who would be a good mother and wife. I needed someone who shared my views on faith and discipline, and who understood the ministry of a football coach. Although my wife is beautiful, her looks, size, shape, hair, color, accent, hobbies or friends were not the most important things to me. Though, the fact that she is not a big spender is a plus.

I am blessed because although we all need money, money has not become my God. It doesn't dictate my decisions. I don't have any hobbies (which often become a huge drain on finances), and I don't like to shop or take vacations. Therefore, I didn't fall into the trap that most people fall into. Most people choose an occupation based on the starting salary. What I have learned is that the more I make, the more I spend. I end up having the same amount of money in my pocket at the end of the day regardless of my yearly income. Financial maturity is one of my weaknesses and an area in which I am growing daily.

I always knew that I wanted a job that I would enjoy and that I could walk away from at any time. However, as I have gotten older and have a family, I have to make decisions based on what's best for us, not what's best for me. This is another aspect of decision making. How will your decision affect others?

Let's say you grew up in traditional Southern home. This home housed a mother, father, two and a half children, and a dog. You all went to church as a family, and you always did the right thing, and made good grades. In college you realize you are homosexual. Do you "come out"? How does that affect the rest of your family? Does it matter?

What if you are a wife and mother with a beautiful family, but you fall in love with another man? You love your children and your husband, but you are looking for more in a relationship. What do you do? How will your decision affect the rest of your family?

Life is hard.

I try and use these steps before making tough decisions:

1. Pray. I am a man of faith, and I believe prayer works.

2. Identify the problem in words. Actually write it down.

3. Consider my choices. What options do I have?

4. Make a list of pros and cons or positives and negatives for each option or choice.

5. Consult with unbiased people whom I trust, of different backgrounds, who have no dog in the fight.

6. Study people who have made the decision before me. Try to talk to them if I can.

7. Take my time. A rushed decision is usually not the best decision.

8. Take action and don't look back.

# WEDNESDAY

"The weak can never forgive. Forgiveness is the attribute of the strong."

Mahatma Gandhi

## IT IS WISE TO FORGIVE

*There was a family walking along the beach one summer, enjoying the sand, sun, salt, and waves. The little boy slowed the group down because he picked up every shell he could along the way. As they walked and looked out into the Pacific Ocean they noticed a nice big starfish. The father instructed his son to go out and get it. The little boy ran out into the water full speed and once he was half way there he turned around and ran back. The father asked, "Why didn't you keep going?"*

*Before the little boy could catch his breath and answer, the father pushed him back into the water to try again. This time the boy was three steps away before he came back. The father thought his son was afraid of the water going over his head. He assured the boy that he was right behind him, so there was no reason to fear. The little boy ran toward the starfish one more time. He was right there, so close... he reached out, but didn't grab the starfish.*

*On his way back, his father was screaming, "Son, why? Why didn't you just grab it? It was right there, you were so close. All you had to do was grab it." The father got down on one knee and he looked his son in the eye and asked him, "Son, why didn't you grab the starfish?"*

*The son responded, "I tried, but my hands are full of shells."*

We cannot move on with life and grab what's out there if we hold on to anger and resentment. We must forgive, and let go of those negative emotions if we wish to move forward. When we don't forgive, we are imprisoning ourselves. When we hold grudges, it can actually cause our bodies physical damage. No one benefits when we don't forgive.

It is wise to forgive. It is smart. It is the best policy. Most times, when it is hard for us to forgive, the person doesn't deserve forgiving. How can you forgive someone who lied to your face? How can you forgive someone who stole from you or hurt someone you love? I forgive for the same reason I visit my aunt in the nursing home.

People think I visit my aunt because I am a good Christian person or because I love my aunt so much. Neter Mae Wheeler is my great-aunt. She didn't raise me. I didn't even see her much when I was growing up. I live over 100 miles away from her nursing home, but I visit her more than any other family member for one reason. I want someone to visit me if I am ever in a nursing home. That is why I forgive. If I ever do anything intentional or on accident that causes someone harm, I want them to forgive me.

Forgiving someone is more for you than for the other person. They probably don't even know you have a problem with them. When you forgive, you experience freedom. When you don't forgive, when you harbor anger, bitterness, resentment, or hatred toward someone else, that stress hurts you emotionally and physically. When you let go of these emotions, you dramatically reduce your stress levels. In order to experience the benefits of forgiveness, you must first decide to forgive.

Forgiveness is a choice. Forgiveness takes effort. The decision to forgive is rational and logical. We can't wait until we *feel* like it, because that may never happen. Once the decision to forgive is made, your behavior will change in a positive way toward the person you've forgiven. However, forgiving the person is different and entirely separate from forgiving their actions. Forgiving a person for what they did does not mean you condone the act. It is wise to forgive, but forgetting hurtful actions can prove foolish. If someone stole your money, you need to forgive them, but you don't need to leave your purse by them. Forgiving does not mean forgetting. There is no need to treat the person badly; however, you must exercise common sense.

Forgiving is a process, not a single act. Learning to forgive is a life skill, and it takes time to develop. An integral part of the process is to learn to forgive yourself. Sometimes the hardest person to forgive is yourself, but you can't truly forgive others until you forgive yourself.

What are you waiting for? Are you prepared to take action and forgive that undeserving person?

# THURSDAY

"We cannot become what we need by remaining what we are."

John Maxwell

## LEADERS NEED A POURER

I started waiting tables when I was a teenager. I started my server career at a restaurant called Po' Folks where we served sweet tea out of mason jars and ended my career as a sever at different four star restaurants on Panama City Beach where we poured red and white wine out of expensive wine bottles.

All servers know that the best way to increase your tip is to keep the customers' glass full. I don't care if you are waiting on a diehard NASCAR fan at a mom-and-pop buffet or a plastic surgeon at a five-star restaurant. Nobody likes to run low. You don't want your cell phone battery to run low, or your gas gauge on empty, or your bank account close to zero. How do we avoid this from happening? How do we stay full?

If you are a customer in a restaurant, you motion to your server and ask for a refill. If you are driving your gas-guzzling SUV, you pull up to the gas station and use your card to spend up to a hundred dollars. Most people plug their cell phone in when they go to sleep so that they will have a good charge to take them though the next day. However, we are on our phones so much that we have to have a charger in the car and one at work as well. Our phones have become that important.

If it is vital to keep our cars full of gas, our phones charged, and our glasses full of tea, shouldn't we want to fill up neurologically? Shouldn't we want to fill up our brains, as well? We should want to be in front and not in the rear. We should want to be leaders not followers.

I believe everyone is a leader. You are either the leader of your household, a leader on your job, in your church, or in a civic club. You don't have to have a title to be a leader. We all lead in some capacity. If this is true, what do we do when we are on empty? What about the people who lead us?

What if my pastor and my principal led on empty? What if they never went to any conferences or workshops to learn new information? What if students had teachers who felt they knew it all, so they didn't need to hear another speaker or read another book or go to another workshop?

In 2008, I was in a workshop for leaders and the speaker Al Schierbaum changed my view of leadership with one statement. He said that we can only lead out of the overflow. As a husband, father, speaker, author, teacher, and coach I cannot give people what they need if I don't have anything in the reservoir. The closer I get to the bottom, the worse it is for the recipient.

I speak best after I've read a new book. I treat my wife better after I have spent time reading the Bible. I play with my children more after I have watched a documentary about a preacher or coach who spent more time reaching the world than they did reaching their own children. I need to recharge, refill, re-load. When it comes to my cell phone, I don't wait until it gets low to charge it. I try to keep it charged. Likewise, we should recharge our mental and spiritual reservoirs before they are depleted.

I have discovered that the only way I can be an effective leader is to create a lifestyle of learning. I shouldn't wait until my marriage is on the brink of divorce before I try to be a better husband. I shouldn't wait until they threaten my job to start showing up on time. I shouldn't wait until I have an engagement to speak at a church to start reading my Bible.

For me to be the best I can be, to keep my reservoirs full, I had to cut things and people out of my life. My goal is to go from good to great. Not from ok to better, or mediocre to alright. I want to be great, and for me that meant doing some pruning. I don't partake in a lot of empty entertainment. I read one book every month. I write down questions to ask people I admire and respect, and when the opportunity presents itself, I pick their brains. I want to be plugged in to the charger all the time. I want to learn more even when I am not trying to learn more. Although I am not always "on," I am always a leader.

It is hard for leaders to always be "on." Can you imagine your priest or pastor in his boxer shorts, no shirt, drinking a Dr. Pepper and burping loudly in his hallway? Can you imagine the person you admire letting their hair down and being normal?

Whenever an elementary student sees her teacher in the store, she freaks out. She can't believe that Ms. Jones is on the soap aisle, and she is buying soap. The student does not see the teacher or leader as a normal person. The student has never thought of the teacher in a normal context. She has always thought of her as a teacher.

However, we all know the teacher is a person who does normal things like shop for soap. In order for the teacher to reach her full potential, she has to be abnormal in that she must seek out opportunities to stay full in an effort to add value to others. Leaders must continue learning and continue looking out for the interest of others. It is a full-time job that great leaders embrace.

As a leader you have a great responsibility. The Apostle Paul told the church at Philippi to not look out for their own interests, but to look out for the interest of others. Be mindful that everyone is watching. Give them something they can use in a positive way. The world is dark. Be a light.

# FRIDAY

"The purpose of life is to live it, to taste experience to the utmost, to reach out eagerly and without fear for newer and richer experience."

Eleanor Roosevelt

## LIFE IS GREAT!

When thinking of going from good to great, I want you to imagine that you're a cell phone. Imagine you're an old cell phone, the big one like Zack Morris used on the show *Saved by the Bell*. For some of you, an old cell phone would be a flip phone, but I still remember when the flip phone was cool. Believe it or not, when I was in high school and in college, I didn't know many people with a cell phone. As I think back, I remember getting my first cell phone. Having a cell phone at all was a good thing, but having a smart phone is a great thing.

Going from good to great is like going from a Razor to a Galaxy, from the first Blackberry to an iPhone 6. Going from good to great is like going from Myspace to Facebook, from a Discman to an MP3 player. This book is your upgrade. Think of each nugget as an app. I have apps on my phone that I use and apps that I don't use.

What if I only used my phone as a calling and texting device? Or, what if I paid my monthly bill and only used my phone as a calculator? That would be foolish. I think it would be foolish of you not to try and work on some of the nuggets in this book.

I don't think that you have yet come close to reaching your potential. There is so much more in you than you are giving to the world. You can sing, draw, coordinate, decorate, dance, hunt, fish, paint, run, and you are smart. You should team those talents with the everyday wisdom of this resource.

My friend Mark is terminal. My cousin is serving a life sentence. Their attitude toward their situation makes me feel horrible for complaining about my troubles and my issues. I want to live a great life, don't you? I want to have a lifestyle change that cultivates an environment of growth. Growth can't happen unless our environment is conducive to growth.

Snowmen aren't built in Miami, and oranges don't grow in Michigan because their environment isn't conducive to growth. Sometimes our work environment and even our home situation are not set up for us to grow. We have to change the environment we are in or find a way to spend most of our time elsewhere. Death is a part of life, but so is growth. If you spend your time in the Valley of Death, you will have a hard time growing. However, if we spend time with positive people who value life, we may experience growth. We may experience life, not death.

I go home to attend funerals quite often. Our family always uses the same funeral home, and subsequently, I have gotten to know the funeral home director. He greets me with the same greeting every time.

"It's good to see you again," he says.

In the most respectful way possible I say, "No, it's not good to see you again."

By now, I am sure he knows that I am just teasing him, but every time I see him someone has died. For the sake of this analogy let's say he represents death. Is there anyone in your life that represents death? Not actual death, but is there someone who represents death in your lifestyle or environment? Death in your career, social, or personal life? Life is great when we are in the right environment.

A friend of mine is a pastor and a mortician. What do you think is going through his mind when business at the funeral home is slow and he has to visit an elderly member in the hospital? Is he going to pray for the member to be healed? Is he going to pray for the member to find their eternal rest in heaven? What is his motive? Is he trying to make money or is he trying to comfort his church member? He may think he can do both. What a dilemma.

I'm just kidding. The truth is there are people out there who do mean you harm. Those people don't need to be in your life. When my grandmother would bake a casserole or a cake in the kitchen, she would tell us to not go in the kitchen because we may make it fall. We have to keep the wrong type of people out of our lives so that the things we have cooking will rise and turn out well.

Life is good when we wake up, go through the day, and merely exist. Life is great when we are intent on transforming daily. Like Optimus Prime and Megatron, we can transform. We can change from the way we are into something different and, possibly, better. A loose definition of foolishness, stupidity, or insanity is doing the same thing over and over again and expecting different results.

If we want to go from good to great, we must have a paradigm shift. We must get outside our comfort zone. If we do what we've always done, we will have what we've always had. I am thankful for a good life. However, I am looking forward to going from a good life to a great life!

# Weekend Application

The goal is to pick two of the five items we discussed this week and make an effort to go from good to great in that area. After deciding which two you want to focus on, formulate a plan of action. Then ask yourself *What am I going to do each day to accomplish my goal?* Be sure to chart your progress and reward yourself periodically.

## Monday- What don't you want to be when you grow up?

I know I don't want to be average. I don't want to be normal. I don't want to be ordinary. You may not want to be like your father or your mother or your brother or your sister. Write down what you don't want to be and formulate a plan to make sure you succeed.

## Tuesday- Decision Making

Life is full of tough decisions. Is there a big decision you are facing? Try working it out through the decision making process.

## Wednesday- It is Wise to Forgive

The hardest part about forgiving is actually doing it. Send the person you need to forgive a text, a phone call, or an email. Better yet, meet with them face to face and say I forgive you. You can't control their response, but you can experience freedom by forgiving.

## Thursday- Leaders Need a Pourer

Who is leading the leaders? Who can the leaders talk to? You're a leader. We all are. We all need to be recharged and rejuvenated. Make a decision to stay plugged in.

## Friday- Life is Great!

Life can be great! Make a list of things that are holding you back from being the best that you can be. Pick one to conquer. How do you eat an elephant? One bite at a time. We're like Home Depot. We believe you can do it, and we believe we can help.

# TRANSFORMING YOUR LIFE FROM GOOD TO GREAT: DAILY NUGGETS OF WISDOM